Power to rise above any crisis:

# WORSHIP THROUGH THE STORM

'Based on a prophetic vision'

## Eku McGred

Cover designed by Samuel Alebioshu

Published by:

McDougal & Associates

18896 Greenwell Springs Road

Greenwell Springs, Louisiana 70739

www.ThePublishedWord.com

For information contact Oblango Edutainment,
speedmusicsolutions@rocketmail.com

ISBN 978-1-934769-98-0

Printed on demand in the UK, the US and Australia

# Dedication

I dedicate this book to all those going through hard times, those caught in the eye of life's stormy season.

# Acknowledgements

Thanks to God and all of the people who have helped and supported me through my season of storm. This book is a fruit of your investment.

# Contents

# Section IV: Worshipping through the Storm

# Section V: The Conclusion

# Preface

Thank God for storms. It was a storm that woke me up from my slumber, and it caused me to arise in the area of my gifting. The storm of life hit so hard that I was literally knocked out of my comfort zone, but it sent me into the path of discovering my purpose in life. This book is in your hand today because it is part of God's purpose for me to pass this message along to you and for you to be one of those who will be receiving it.

At some point, every one of us will face situations that shake us to the core, challenges that put everything we have and everything we know to the test. These circumstances stretch us to the breaking point, threatening to destroy our very foundation, even our faith. These are usually the most uncomfortable periods of our lives, periods in which the demands of life are at their highest but our resources – both physical and spiritual– seem to be at their lowest. These are the situations and circumstances that are referred to as a storm within this book.

As you continue reading through the rest of this book you will begin to have a clearer understanding as to the reasons why God seems to allow us to go through these difficult times, even when we have been faithfully pursuing His will and purpose for our lives. It will also help to enrich your understanding of the many dimensions of worship, as well as its necessity whilst going through a storm. We will be exploring its depth, width and height.

My sincere hope is that even in your current challenge you will learn to worship God, and as you worship Him, you will begin to find the treasures that He has hidden for you within the storm. Not only that, but as you worship you will discover God's heart towards you and your heart towards Him.

This book will not only open your eyes to see these storms as opportunities to worship God. It will also help you develop a better understanding of what it really means to worship God in spirit and in truth.

# Section I

# Why Worship through the Storm?

# Chapter 1

# Gifts and Talents

*⁷ But to each one of us grace was given according to the measure of Christ's gift. ⁸ Therefore He says: "When He ascended on high, He led captivity captive, and gave gifts to men."*

**– Ephesians 4:7-8 (NKJV)**

Anytime the word *worship* is mentioned, the first thing that comes to mind is the singing of songs. For most Christians, worship has not only been relegated to singing, it is also thought of as being the preserve of those gifted in the area of music. Worship is much more than songs, performance or rituals. It is the wilful alignment of our heart with the Spirit of God within us and the corresponding actions that manifest in the physical as a result. We worship God through what we do in honour of Him.

Gifts and talents are unique abilities that we naturally possess that enable us to easily excel at certain tasks or activities. These are given to us by God in order to equip us to serve. In serving, we use our gifts and talents in ways that honour God and benefit other people.

# WORSHIP THROUGH THE STORM

God has endowed every one of us with the ability to worship Him. He has not only gifted every one of us with the ability to serve but also to worship through our service. When we use these unique gifts and talents, we worship. This means we do not need the gift of music in order to worship God. Each of us has been specially gifted and talented to worship through that which we have been given. God expects us to worship Him through our service and not limit our worship to the singing of songs, to performances or to empty rituals. The ultimate form of worship is expressed through service. Serving our gifts and talents to God first and then serving it to humanity.

From this passage in Ephesians 4:7-8, we learn that we have all been given gifts by God. But, often times, these gifts and talents are buried so deep within us that it takes something outside of ourselves – such as parents, teachers, mentors or storms – to draw them out of us. Storms provide us with the best opportunity for discovering hidden gifts and talents, by allowing us to look much deeper within ourselves than we normally would. They enable us to draw up from the well of the undiscovered, undeveloped, underutilized – and sometimes ignored – natural skills and abilities.

Many of us are aware of a primary gift or talent we possess and we dismiss others. However, through storms, God enables us to uncover the deep– seated qualities embedded within us. The experience forces us to look and venture out much further than we have previously done.

## Dreams and Visions

After serving in the music department in the church for over a decade, I had convinced myself that this was the only gift I had been given by God with which I could serve my local church. And I did so faithfully. However, subconsciously I was dismissing the other gifts and talents that lay deep below the surface. One of those was the gift of dreams and visions.

*²⁸ And afterward, I will pour out my Spirit on all people. Your sons and daughters will prophesy, your old men will dream dreams, your young men will see visions.*

**Joel 2:28**

It took a very long time for me to realize the significance of dreams and visions and to recognize that I am in a privileged position to have been given these gifts by God. Without the Scriptures, we can ignore the very gifts and talents God has given us to be a blessing to our world. Lacking this insight, our natural tendency is to ignore the minor gifts – those that are seemingly insignificant, boring or uncelebrated.

Each of us has been given a gift and commissioned by Jesus. Until we arise and start using our gifts and talents we will be ignoring the very things God has given us to be a blessing to our world.

*¹⁵ He said to them, "Go into all the world and preach the gospel to all creation.*
*¹⁶ Whoever believes and is baptized will be saved, but whoever does not believe will be condemned. ¹⁷ And these signs will accompany those who believe: In my name they will drive out demons; they will speak in new tongues; ¹⁸ they will pick up snakes with their hands; and when they drink deadly poison, it will not hurt them at all; they will place their hands on sick people, and they will get well."*

**Mark 16:15-18**

In the next chapter, I will share with you the prophetic vision of worship God showed me, a vision about the incredible power that we have available within us, a power this is only released when we learn to worship through the storm.

I have made the decision to be a good steward of all the gifts and talents God has given me and to obey and follow Him as He leads. This book you are now reading is a direct result of that obedience. It is not in your hand by chance, but by divine orchestration. So I implore you to receive this message and to allow the Holy Spirit to help you put into practice that which the Father is saying to us through the revelation contained in this book.

The Bible admonish us to test every spirit to see whether they be of God, therefore I admonish you to put the message contained in this book to the test and see whether it is of God.

[1] *Beloved, do not believe every spirit, but test the spirits, whether they are of God; because many false prophets have gone out into the world.*

**1 John 4:1 (NKJV)**

Like the apostle Paul, I have made up my mind not to be disobedient to the heavenly vision. As you receive this revelation and put it into practice, the results will speak for themselves.

[19] *"So then, King Agrippa, I was not disobedient to the vision from heaven.... ."*
**Acts 26:19**

# Chapter 2

# A Prophetic Vision of Worship

*[14] For God may speak in one way, or in another, yet man does not perceive it. [15] In a dream, in a vision of the night, when deep sleep falls upon men, while slumbering on their beds, [16] Then He opens the ears of men, and seals their instruction.*

## – Job 33:14-16 (NKJV)

There are different kinds of visions and they come in various forms. The major kinds are: spiritual visions, trances and open visions. Spiritual visions are visions in which you see with your spiritual eye, not your physical eye. Your spiritual eye is the eye of your spirit; it is the eye you use to see pictures in dreams when you are asleep. The apostle Paul had such vision on the Damascus road (see Acts 9). In a trance, one's physical senses are in suspense – you are more conscious of spiritual things than the physical things that may be going on around you. You are caught up in a dream– like experience, but you are not sleeping. Cornelius's vision in Acts 10 falls under this kind of vision. Finally, there is open vision, where one's physical senses are intact and eyes wide open. The prophet Ezekiel had such vision when he was standing by the river Chebar in Ezekiel 1.

In every one of the examples I sighted above, there was a remarkable change in the life of the people involved and also in those whom they were sent to deliver. The apostle Paul, in obedience to his heavenly vision, not only regained his sight, but also went on to make a lasting impact on the world around him. The same could be said of Cornelius, who became the first gentile to receive the baptism of the Holy Spirit and the prophet Ezekiel, who foretold the fate of the nation of Israel many generations in advance.

The vision I am about to share with you came to me in the form of a dream; it was a form of spiritual vision, the kind of vision referred to in scripture as a *'vision of the night,'* the same kind of vision we find in the book of Daniel 7.

*[1] In the first year of Belshazzar king of Babylon, Daniel had a dream and visions of his head while on his bed. Then he wrote down the dream, telling the main facts.*
**Daniel 7:1 (NKJV)**

## A Vision of Worship

In my dream I saw myself in what looked like a stadium. I was standing on the field – the lowest part of the stadium – and there were two levels above me. On the first level, I saw a figure that was in the form of a man, and on the level above that, I saw numerous people standing. It seemed as if they were spectators looking down on what was happening on the field, and although I could not make out their faces, I knew they were there. I saw them looking on. Their image looked like a silhouette.

As I looked, I could sense within myself that the figure that was standing on the first level was devilish, so I began to pray. I was praying earnestly and fervently against it, using all the warfare prayers against danger I knew. I was calling on the name of Jesus, pleading the blood of Jesus, calling down the fire of the Holy Ghost, yet it seemed that none of my prayers were effective against this evil presence. Instead of the prayers instantaneously getting rid of this figure, what I noticed was that the whole time I was praying the figure kept laughing. The harder I prayed, the harder the figure continued to laugh.

Then, suddenly, I sensed God's presence appearing in the open sky above the stadium. I looked up, and as I did I instantaneously started worshipping. As I worshiped, I felt myself being lifted up. It appeared to me as if I was levitating towards the presence of a bright, white light. I felt my body rising above the place I was standing, and my heart felt an unquantifiable measure of peace and joy.

The more I worshipped the higher I rose, and the closer I got to the light of God's presence that was above the stadium. The intensity of the light got brighter and brighter the closer I got, and the peace and joy I felt was also exponentially increasing. The feeling was wonderful – nothing else on earth can come close to comparing to it.

I continued ascending as I kept on worshipping till I reached a crescendo. I was now above the stadium where God's presence was. At this point an overwhelming feeling of love, joy and peace – all rolled up into one – had filled me up so completely that it felt as if I was about to explode.

## The Vision's Explanation

Many times the imagery seen in dreams and visions is symbolic, so I had to do what Daniel did: I took time aside to study the Scriptures and to pray for God to open the eyes of my understanding so that I could understand the meaning of the dream.

*15 And it came to pass, when I, even I Daniel, had seen the vision, and sought for the meaning, then, behold, there stood before me as the appearance of a man.*

**Daniel 8:15 (KJV)**

As with any vision, it is usually multi-layered, therefore, as one's level of understanding increases, deeper revelations of the various aspects of the vision will be uncovered. At this point in time, I hereby present to you my current understanding of the meaning of this vision as it relates to worshipping God through the storms of life.

The **field** where I was standing in this dream represents the earth – the lowest of the three levels. We find the earth being mentioned as God's footstool, the level He has chosen for His footrest.

*48 Howbeit the most High dwelleth not in temples made with hands; as saith the prophet, 49 Heaven is my throne, and earth is my footstool: what house will ye build me? saith the Lord: or what is the place of my rest? 50 Hath not my hand made all these things?*

**Acts 7:48-50 (KJV)**

The **first level,** where the devilish figure was standing, represents the first heaven. The first heaven is the space directly above the earth. It includes the air and planetary space. This is the place where Satan and the other fallen angels reside, and from where they tirelessly fight against God's children on earth.

*13 But the prince of the kingdom of Persia withstood me one and twenty days: but, lo, Michael, one of the chief princes, came to help me; and I remained there with the kings of Persia.*

**Daniel 10:13 (KJV)**

*12 Therefore rejoice, ye heavens, and ye that dwell in them. Woe to the inhabiters of the earth and of the sea! for the devil is come down unto you, having great wrath, because he knoweth that he hath but a short time.*

**Revelation 12:12 (KJV)**

*2 Wherein in time past ye walked according to the course of this world, according to the prince of the power of the air, the spirit that now worketh in the children of disobedience.*

**Ephesians 2:2 (KJV)**

The **second level** of the stadium I saw in the vision represents the second heaven. It is representative of the place the Lord has prepared for those who love Him and are called according to His purpose. It is where the saints who have gone on to be with the Lord await. They are the great cloud of witnesses standing in heaven, looking on as we engage the devil in spiritual combat.

*1 Therefore, since we are surrounded by such a great cloud of witnesses, let us throw off everything that hinders and the sin that so easily entangles. And let us run with perseverance the race marked out for us, 2 fixing our eyes on Jesus, the pioneer and perfecter of faith. For the joy set before him he endured the cross, scorning its shame, and sat down at the right hand of the throne of God. 3 Consider him who endured such opposition from sinners, so that you will not grow weary and lose heart.*

**Hebrews 12:1-3**

In the vision, **the sky above** the stadium, where God's presence was, represents the third heaven, the place where God dwells. Unlike the first and second levels, where God's presence appeared over the stadium had no confinement. From where I was standing I could see that it was the entire expanse of the sky. This was to show that God is not just in a different dimension, but that He is also in a dimension far superior to anything that exists in the rest of creation. It speaks of His limitlessness and His omnipotence.

# WORSHIP THROUGH THE STORM

*¹⁴ Behold, the heaven and the heaven of heavens is the LORD's thy God, the earth also, with all that therein is.*

**Deuteronomy 10:14 (KJV)**

The figure I saw in the vision standing on the first level laughing as I prayed is figurative of the devil standing in the atmospheric heavens. His laughter represents the storms that he releases against God's children on earth. Our prayers don't seem to be effective against him during the storm because it is his hour. Here is what Jesus said in Luke 22, when the devil released his greatest storm against Him:

*⁵ ³When I was daily with you in the temple, ye stretched forth no hands against me: but this is your hour, and the power of darkness.*

**Luke 22:53 (KJV)**

## A Strategy for Victory

The message that this vision conveys is that our strategy for victory, as children of God, is found in our worship. Most often when we are confronted with challenges, we engage in prayer and assume the devil will just pack up and leave. In actual fact, the opposite is often the case; the more we pray the harder the devil intensifies his fight against us. Therefore our strategy for victory against the devil should not only be to pray, but to also keep our eyes on Jesus and worship Him through the storm. The most effective prayer we can ever pray is one that is preceded by worship.

Worship brings us to the position in God where all prayers are answered. We can see this in Matthew 6, where Jesus set out a model of prayer for us:

*⁹ In this manner, therefore, pray:* **Our Father in heaven, hallowed be Your name.** *¹⁰ Your kingdom come. Your will be done on earth as it is in heaven. ¹¹ Give us this day our daily bread. ¹² And forgive us our debts, As we forgive our debtors. ¹³ And do not lead us into temptation, But deliver us from the evil one. For Yours is the kingdom and the power and the glory forever. Amen.*

**Matthew 6:9-13 (NKJV)**

In this model prayer, worship came first: *"our Father in heaven hallowed be Your name."* If we are to pray and have our prayers readily answered, then our strategy must be to adopt the pattern of prayer Jesus revealed to us.

In the vision I saw myself fervently praying, the dread of pending calamity spurring me on. But I was praying mostly out of fear rather than out of faith and trust in God's Word. My mouth was filled with words of desperation rather than words of confidence in God's omnipotent power and ability.

Things took a different turn the moment I perceived the presence of God above the stadium and looked up. What happened was that when I looked up, my focus changed. I was no longer looking at the storm and, instead, my eyes became fixed on Jesus, the Author and Finisher of my faith. That change in perspective resulted in a change in the words that were coming out of my mouth. Instead of uttering desperate words of prayer, I was now declaring faith-filled words of worship. Consequently, I saw myself rising above the circumstances that surrounded me.

*² Looking unto Jesus the author and finisher of our faith; who for the joy that was set before him endured the cross, despising the shame, and is set down at the right hand of the throne of God.*

**Hebrews 12:2 (KJV)**

Without faith it is impossible to worship God through the storm. Whenever we chose to worship God in the midst of difficulties and challenges, we are expressing our belief,

WORSHIP THROUGH THE STORM

confidence and trust in God's omnipotence. This is when God's power starts working within us, and the presence of the Holy Spirit is made manifest around us. The only way we can rise above any storm is to keep our focus on Jesus. This truth is best illustrated by the apostle in the book of Matthew 14:

*²⁹ So He said, "Come." And when Peter had come down out of the boat, he walked on the water to go to Jesus. ³⁰ But when he saw that the wind was boisterous, he was afraid; and beginning to sink he cried out, saying, "Lord, save me!"*

**Matthew 14:29-30 (NKJV)**

As long as Peter kept his eyes on Jesus, he kept walking on the water, but the moment his focus changed, he started to sink. In the same way that Peter kept on walking on the water, as long as his eyes were fixed on Jesus, so it was in the vision. As I kept worshipping God, I kept moving upward and higher towards God's presence.

As we keep our eyes on Jesus, we lose sight of what is going on around us. Thus, we are able to express our faith, love, appreciation, and dependence on God through worship. This is what causes a release of the power of God already within us. This is the power that enabled Peter to walk on water, and it is the same power which will move us upwards and higher, until we are enthroned with Christ Jesus far above the storms.

*⁶ and raised us up together, and made us sit together in the heavenly places in Christ Jesus.*

**Ephesians 2:6 (NKJV)**


## How the Vision Relates to Us

How does this relate to us? Well, you see, all of Creation, including the saints who have gone to be with the Lord, are looking on in eager anticipation of our victory over the devil.

In just the same way we would look and cheer on our favourite football team, when they are playing against an opposing side, so also the saints in heaven. They are excitedly anticipating our triumph on earth.

Though I did not see anything other than the saints standing there and looking on, I do believe they rejoice together with us. I am convinced that in the same way they rejoice for the salvation of one sinner, so also they rejoice as we continue to fight the good fight of faith. They celebrate as we worship God through whatever storm we are facing – joblessness, foreclosures, sickness, loss, pain, suffering etc.

Through this vision, the Father is telling us not only that our victory is found in worship, but also that all of the saints in heaven are eagerly looking on as we defeat the enemy's power through worship. Does this mean there is no need to pray? No! We need to pray, but most of our prayer time should be spent in worshipping God. Spend time thanking God for answers to prayers and express that confidence through worship.

Worship is more valuable when offered in the eye of a storm than when offered from the comfort of normality. The greatest and most challenging periods of our lives provide us with the opportunity to offer unto God our most valuable treasure – our worship.

As you continue reading this book, you will discover that this vision not only conveys a message about worship, but also about the power we have available to us when we worship through a storm. Furthermore, it will expand and deepen your understanding of what it means to truly worship.

# Section II

# What Is Worship About?

# Chapter 3

# The True Meaning of Worship

[23] *But the time is coming — indeed it's here now — when true worshipers will worship the Father in spirit and in truth. The Father is looking for those who will worship him that way.*

*– John 4:23 (NLT)*

It was testimony time, and I was ministering a song I wrote called *"You Gave Me a Song through the Storm."* After I had finished ministering the song, a lady walked up and told the church how armed robbers had attacked her family and shot her brother several times. Her brother had not died from the attack, but was lying in the intensive care unit of a hospital in a very critical state, with a very slim possibility that he would survive. The situation was grim. Now she was confronted with a very difficult choice. She could choose to either continue wallowing in her feeling of grief and helplessness, or she could choose to break out of that gloom by worshipping God with a song.

It seemed there was no reason for her to be in a worshipful mood, let alone to be singing a song. Nevertheless she began to sing. The main section of the lyrics of the song I was teaching the church says:

31

# WORSHIP THROUGH THE STORM

*You gave me a song through the storm*
*A song of praise to Your name*
*And as I wait I worship You.*

That day, this lady made a choice, she chose to worship God through the storm. She made the right choice and sang a song of praise to God, giving Him worship. The decision she made and the actions that resulted from that one decision is what true worship is all about.

## A Definition of True Worship

Worship goes beyond the songs that we sing with our mouths, to the songs that proceed from our heart. True worship can be defined as the outward expression of the decisions of our heart, the manifestation of what is truly going on in our spirit towards God.

*8 These people draw near to Me with their mouth, And honour Me with their lips, but their heart is far from Me. 9 And in vain they worship Me, Teaching as doctrines the commandments of men."*

**Matthew 15:8-9 (NKJV)**

True worship, as God sees it, is when the worship of our mouth and our hearts agrees with what is coming from our spirit towards Him. When we speak of worship we also speak of giving, of expressing admiration, appreciation, gratitude and honour towards God.

God derives immense pleasure from our worship. When we direct our worship towards Him, we are functioning as He designed us, and He is pleased by that. Just like a new father would look over his child and feel great pride and pleasure, so also it is with God. His greatest joy is experiencing us worship Him – just being our true and original selves.

Worship is also an attitude – a way of thinking, feeling, giving and living – that we can adopt. It is an attitude of expressing worth, confidence and emotion towards God. Worship is about paying great honour or respect. It is about putting ourselves in the position of willing subjection to God's will and purpose. Genuine worship is spiritual. It is initiated in the spirit and translated to the heart or soul and is then expressed through our attitude, our way of thinking and acting.

From this definition, we can see that worship is not just a physical act but also a spiritual act as well. This means that physically bowing down in worship and making proclamations is not true worship unless it is in agreement with what is coming from our heart. The actions of prostrating, or singing, must be a direct translation into the physical dimension of the worship that is going on in our heart in honour of God.

All throughout history, we have seen men who have bowed before their king and the next moment stabbed him in the heart. This was the case with Judas. He was outwardly bowing down to his Leader, but inwardly he was stabbing Him. Physically, he was projecting a form of worship towards Jesus, but spiritually his heart was worshipping something else. The physical betrayal that followed was a direct translation into the physical dimension of the kind of worship that was going on in his heart.

Worship is much more than singing songs. It goes beyond attending a service and giving sacrificial offerings. When we truly worship, our worship acts as a doorway that takes us to the consciousness of our spirit, releasing our spirit to commune with God. And because our spirit is divine, we

33

need not instruct it on how or what to do when we worship God. Our spirit is of God, therefore it is programmed to relate with and worship God as He intended. Once the connection is established with our heart, our spirit automatically knows what to do. In the same way, when our hearts make the connection with our mouth, subconsciously what comes out of our mouth will be a translation of what is in our heart.

*34 ...for out of the abundance of the heart the mouth speaks. 35 A good man out of the good treasure of his heart brings forth good things, and an evil man out of the evil treasure brings forth evil things.*

**Matthew 12:34-35 (NJKV)**

When we allow our spirit to connect with God through the Holy Spirit the result is what worship truly is. This is the type of worship that God desires most. It is pure and undiluted. It is worship in the highest dimension and at its highest level. This is the reason why the Scriptures say in John 24:

*24 God is **Spirit**, and those who **worship** Him must **worship in spirit** and truth.*

**John 4:24 (NKJV)**

To worship God in truth means our mouth and our heart agreeing with what is coming from our spirit, i.e. the body and soul (mind, will and intellect) in sync with our spirit – quickened and made alive by the Holy Spirit.

True worship is expressed not only in our physical demeanour or rituals, but also in our heart's attitude toward God. Whenever worship is out of line with the decision of our heart, that worship is vain. From the above scripture we can see that whatever qualifies as true worship must be in agreement with the whole of our being: spirit, soul and body. So what comes out of our lips should line up with what we think, do and say.

To know whether our worship is vain or not we can put it through the test of the heart. When our heart worships, everything else flows easily; our mouth lines up with our heart, which, in turn, lines up with our spirit, which links up with the Holy Spirit.

You can usually tell when this is not the case. Worship then becomes a boring, empty and tiresome ritual with an attitude that says: worship is what we have to do in order to satisfy God.

I should also mention that worship is not always easy or exciting. There are times when true worship will demand the sacrifice of our comfort. In Genesis 22, the patriarch Abraham was asked by God to worship Him with that which was most dear to his heart – his only son Isaac. The obedience he demonstrated was a direct translation – into the physical dimension – of the decision of his heart. He had made the decision to offer God true worship.

[17] *By faith Abraham, when he was tested, offered up Isaac, and he who had received the promises offered up his only begotten son,* [18] *of whom it was said, "In Isaac your seed shall be called,"* [19] *concluding that God was able to raise him up, even from the dead, from which he also received him in a figurative sense.*

## Hebrews 11:17-19 (NKJV)

Abraham's worship was expressed through his obedience. Let us now go to the next chapter, where we will look at the various expressions of worship.

# Chapter 4

# Expressions of Worship

*²Let my prayer be set before You as incense,*
*The lifting up of my hands as the evening sacrifice.*

**–Psalm 141:2 (NKJV)**

To escape the snare of saying lots of words and doing lots of actions but ascribing very little of worth to God we must realize that true worship is a spiritual exercise. For worship to be of any worth to God, it has to be expressed in ways that make spiritual sense. What this means is that we have to express our worship in ways that produce significant spiritual worth. And the only means through which we are able to do that is through the expression of the gifts and fruits of the Spirit.

The most important of these gifts and fruits are faith, hope and love. These three qualities turn out to be the three abiding attitudes of the heart that facilitate true worship.

*¹ Though I speak with the tongues of men and of angels, but have not love, I have become sounding brass or a clanging cymbal. ² And though I have the gift of prophecy, and understand all mysteries and all knowledge, and though I have all*

# WORSHIP THROUGH THE STORM

*faith, so that I could remove mountains, but have not love, I am nothing … .*
*[13] And now abide faith, hope, love, these three; but the greatest of these is love.*

**1 Corinthians 13:1-13 (NKJV)**

We ourselves have to become a living sacrifice. And we become a living sacrifice by making the conscious decision in our hearts to physically express and live out the gifts and fruits of the Holy Spirit of God within us.

*[1] Therefore, I urge you, brothers and sisters, in view of God's mercy, to offer your bodies as a living sacrifice, holy and pleasing to God — this is your true and proper worship.*

**Romans 12:1**

We offer our bodies as a living sacrifice by living out our faith, expressing our love and holding onto our hope. In essence, worship that is honouring to God is the outward expression of an inward worship. But this takes the empowerment of our spirit through the Holy Spirit to get us to the place where we offer truly our bodies as a living sacrifice.

Worship that is aimed at pleasing God must transcend the dimension of body and soul; it must be from the spirit. This means that its origin and destination must be in agreement for it to be true worship – spirit to Spirit. Spirit calls out to spirit, just as deep calls out to deep. God is a spirit, and if we are to call out to Him in worship, it has to be the spiritual exercise of offering ourselves wholly to Him – body, soul and spirit , for that is the expression of true worship.

*[24] For God is a Spirit and they that worship him must worship him in spirit and in truth.*

**John 4:24 (KJV)**

With the help of the Holy Spirit we can come to the place of true worship, the place where our hearts reflect our spirit, and our mouths and actions reflect our hearts. This is when we begin to reflect God's image, becoming a true expression of His very nature.

## Physical and Spiritual Expressions of Worship

There is not only the physical expression of worship, but there is also the spiritual expression of worship. And when it comes to the physical expression of worship, we are only limited by the level of our creativity. There are myriads of ways we can physically express worship, just as there are myriads of way we can express admiration, appreciation, gratitude and honour to someone we love and respect.

Physical beings can only see and experience worship that is expressed in a physical way. In like manner, spiritual beings can only see and experience worship that is expressed in a spiritual way. But we, as humans, are both physical and spiritual in nature. We are physical beings with a spiritual component in us, and so we are able to express worship both physically and spiritually.

All throughout church and biblical history, the physical expression of worship has changed and continues to change. One thing that has not changed is the spiritual expression of worship. What has happened over time is that, at different points in history, there have come deeper revelations and insights into the aspect of what it means to worship in spirit.

Until Jesus came and started teaching on the importance of spiritual worship over physical worship, there was not much said about it. Till then, to have worshiped meant to have performed religious duties as required by the Law. Much of Jesus's life and teaching, when studied, reveals one truth: God is much more interested in us expressing worship spiritually then on allowing that spiritual expression of worship to guide our physical expression of worship.

# WORSHIP THROUGH THE STORM

Jesus expressed true worship (i.e. spiritual worship), by willingly laying down His will to the will of God the Father. He made the conscious choice to deliberately subject the decisions of His heart to the pleasing of the Father.

*39 Going a little farther, he fell with his face to the ground and prayed, "My Father, if it is possible, may this cup be taken from me. Yet not as I will, but as you will."*

**Matthew 26:39**

### FAITH AND LOVE AS EXPRESSIONS OF WORSHIP

Physical expressions – like singing, dancing and fasting – can take on a completely different form when they are expressed in their spiritual equivalents, in forms such as love, faith, obedience, etc.

Love and faith are the best expressions of worship, and one cannot be found without the other. Any worship devoid of love and faith is vain and boils down to flattery. Only hypocrites give worship that is void of value and substance. Any attempt at worship without its constituent components – love and faith – becomes empty and is synonymous with sycophancy.

Spiritual expression of worship should always be accompanied by it physical equivalence. Take the example of faith: Faith as mentioned earlier is one of the three most important spiritual qualities in the expression of true worship. When faith is expressed in the heart, it is spiritual in nature, but when it is expressed in works, it is physical in nature. For faith to be real faith, it has to have both the spiritual component and the physical component – a belief in God followed up by corresponding works. Faith as an example of the expression of true worship is comprised of a belief in the heart that God is and that He rewards those who please Him, which is then backed up by matching physical actions.

*14 What does it profit, my brethren, if someone says he has faith but does not have works? Can faith save him? .... 17 Thus also faith by itself, if it does not have works, is dead.*

## James 2:14-17 (NKJV)

Faith is one way we articulate true worship. It is the practical expression of our confidence in God based on trust in His Word. Our confidence in God is a demonstration of our worship; it gives Him pleasure. Wherever there is faith, fear is dispelled. Without fear we are free to express our worship to God through the deadliest storm. And we are liberated to worship God across all dimensions and levels.

# Chapter 5

# Dimensions and Levels of Worship

*³ For we are the circumcision, who worship God in the Spirit, rejoice in Christ Jesus, and have no confidence in the flesh.*
## – *Philippians 3:3 (NKJV)*

Just as it is foolish to give spiritual worship to physical beings, so also it is foolish to give spiritual beings physical worship. The best way I can illustrate this truth is like this: imagine you are invited to visit a king at his palace. When you get there, you decide to show your honour to the king by standing in front of him and singing of his splendour and majesty, but you decide to do it in your heart. Instead of you displaying your reverence by physically bowing, kneeling or prostrating yourself before the king, you insist on doing it all only in your mind.

Can you get the picture of how ridiculous that is? The king has no ability to read your mind. He is incapable of hearing the beautiful words coming from your heart towards him, because he is in the physical dimension, and you are expressing your worship in the spiritual dimension.

# WORSHIP THROUGH THE STORM

This is exactly what happens when we lack an understanding of the different dimensions of worship. Most of us Christians get caught in the trap of giving God religious [physical] worship instead of the spiritual worship that He most desires from us.

The only worship that really reaches God's throne is spiritual worship, the worship that comes from our spirit. That's why the Scriptures declare in John 4:24, *"God is a Spirit: and they that worship him must worship him in spirit and in truth"* (KJV).

Most people interpret this scripture as saying: *"must worship Him in Spirit,"* when it actually says: *"must worship Him in spirit."* In case you have not noticed the difference, the word *spirit* is in lower case, referring to the human spirit, not in uppercase *Spirit*, which would have been referring to the Holy Spirit.

To worship in truth means to worship from our hearts. When we worship from our heart, our worship is being energized by our spirit. And the worship that comes from our spirit is itself being energized by the Holy Spirit of God within us. Thus, we are enabled to worship in body, soul and spirit.

Mankind was designed by God to function in three dimensions – body, soul and spirit – just as God Himself. Therefore we have been empowered by God to worship at every level and in all three dimensions.

Every form of worship we can ever give to God can be expressed in three dimensions, each of which can be manifested in one of four levels. I have made an attempt to explain this further in the following section (*see diagram 1*).

## Dimensions of Worship

The dimensions and levels of worship are in hierarchical order, from the lowest to the highest. The lowest dimension being *body* and the highest being *spirit*. The lowest level is *vocal* whilst the highest is *value*.

*Diagram 1* shows examples of each dimension and how each is expressed across the four levels.

| | | DIMENSIONS | | |
|---|---|---|---|---|
| | | **Body** | **Soul** | **Spirit** |
| **L E V E L S** | **Vocal** | *Singing* | *Reverence* | *Integrity* |
| | **Choreograph** | *Dancing* | *Obedience* | *Hope* |
| | **Visual** | *Charity* | *Meditation* | *Faith* |
| | **Value** | *Sacrifice* | *Fruitfulness* | *Love* |

*Diagram 1: Levels and Dimension of worship*

### THE FIRST DIMENSION: THE BODY

This is the first and lowest dimension of worship. It is the dimension of worship which deals with the physical realm.

When we worship in this dimension, we use our body in ways that communicate worth to God. Anything we can physically do in honour of God falls under this dimension of worship. Worship at this dimension is usually dictated by our emotional state and prevailing circumstance. When we are feeling good and things are going our way, we worship readily, but when they are not, we find it difficult to worship.

# WORSHIP THROUGH THE STORM

## THE SECOND DIMENSION OF WORSHIP: THE SOUL

This is the second dimension of worship, and it deals with the soul realm. Worship in this dimension is in a higher dimension than worship in the physical dimension but lower than worship in the spiritual dimension.

When we worship in this dimension we worship with our heart. We use our mind, will and intellect in ways that honour God and communicate worth to Him.

At this dimension worship is spurred on by either what is going on in the physical dimension or by what is going on in the spiritual dimension. In other words, the expression of worship in the soul dimension is dominated by which one of the two other dimensions the soul decides to connect to: the spiritual or the physical. Once the connection is made, the soul will connect with the current experience of the spirit or body and interpret and express worship accordingly.


## THE THIRD DIMENSION OF WORSHIP: THE SPIRIT

This is the third and highest dimension of worship, and it deals with the spiritual realm. When we worship in this dimension our spirit is energized and released to communicate worth to God in worship.

At this dimension, worship becomes purely a spiritual exercise. As we submit our will [heart] to the inspiration and leading of our spirit, the Holy Spirit of God, working within us, takes charge. This is when, through His guidance and tutelage, we begin to truly worship God in spirit. Not only that, but our spirit starts giving out instructions to the other two dimensions, as it receives them from the Holy Spirit, resulting in us worshiping in all three dimensions – spirit, soul and body – at the same time.

# Three Dimensional Worship – 3D

Worshipping in all three dimensions is the highest form of worship. When we worship in 3D, we are fulfilling the purpose for which we were created. By ourselves, however, we are incapable of worshiping God at this dimension. The good news is that, with the help of the Holy Spirit, which was made available to us through the death of Jesus Christ, we can once again worship God in spirit and subsequently in all three dimensions.

*[11] And if the Spirit of him who raised Jesus from the dead is living in you, he who raised Christ from the dead will also give life to your mortal bodies because of his Spirit who lives in you.*

**Romans 8:11**

This is the kind of worship that gives God the most pleasure. It is the type of worship the original Adam practiced, and it is the kind of worship God requires of us, His children, we who have been recreated in Christ Jesus. It is in line with this that I believe the apostle Paul was admonishing the believers in Ephesus and Colossae:

*[18] And do not be drunk with wine, in which is dissipation; but be filled with the Spirit, [19] speaking to one another in psalms and hymns and spiritual songs, singing and making melody in your heart to the Lord, [20] giving thanks always for all things to God the Father in the name of our Lord Jesus Christ, [21] submitting to one another in the fear of God.*

**Ephesians 5:18-21 (NKJV)**

*[16] Let the word of Christ dwell in you richly in all wisdom, teaching and admonishing one another in psalms and hymns and spiritual songs, singing with grace in your hearts to the Lord. [17] And whatever you do in word or deed, do all in the name of the Lord Jesus, giving thanks to God the Father through Him.*

**Colossians 3:16-17 (NKJV)**

God is saying the same to us today through the letters the apostle Paul wrote to the Ephesian and Colossian believers, and He is calling us to come up higher in our worship, to start worshipping Him in spirit and in truth and to worship Him through the storm. He wants the worship from His people to cut across all dimensions and become 3D. The only way we can do this is by constantly reminding ourselves of the truth: *God desires worship from our spirit, soul and body.*

King David is a good example of someone who, even though he was living in the Old Testament, practiced worshipping in 3D. In Psalm 103 we find King David talking about three-dimensional worship, worship from his soul, his spirit and from his mouth:

*¹ Praise the LORD, my soul; all my inmost being, praise his holy name.*
*² Praise the LORD, my soul, and forget not all his benefits.*

**Psalm 103:1-2**

Again in Psalm 138 we see David putting 3D worship into practice, honouring God with his body, soul and spirit. He was someone who worshipped through the storm.

*¹ I will praise You with my whole heart; before the gods I will sing praises to You. ² I will worship toward Your holy temple, and praise Your name for Your lovingkindness and Your truth; for You have magnified Your word above all Your name. ³ In the day when I cried out, You answered me, and made me bold with strength in my soul . . . . ⁷ Though I walk in the midst of trouble, You will revive me; You will stretch out Your hand against the wrath of my enemies, and Your right hand will save me. ⁸ The LORD will perfect that which concerns me; Your mercy, O LORD, endures forever; do not forsake the works of Your hands.*

**Psalm 138: 1-8 (NKJV)**

# Levels of Worship

## THE VOCAL LEVEL

Worship at this level involves the use of the voice. At this level, we express our worship through the medium of words or songs.

Any category of sound that is produced by our voice in exultation, honour or appreciation of God falls under this level of worship.

*¹ Make a joyful noise unto the LORD, all ye lands. ² Serve the LORD with gladness: come before his presence with singing. ³ Know ye that the LORD he is God: it is he that hath made us, and not we ourselves; we are his people, and the sheep of his pasture. ⁴ Enter into his gates with thanksgiving, and into his courts with praise: be thankful unto him, and bless his name. ⁵ For the LORD is good; his mercy is everlasting; and his truth endureth to all generations.*

**Psalm 100:1-5 (KJV)**

Naturally, as vocal beings, our voice is physically our most effective form of communication. Therefore our voice provides us the means to communicate worship at its most basic level. The expression of worship at this level is the lowest of all the four levels of worship.

## THE VISUAL LEVEL

Worship at this level involves the use of our mind. We express worship at this level through the medium of thoughts, using our imagination in ways that honour God. Anything that is produced by our mind in exultation, honour or appreciation of God falls under this level of worship. Another word for *worship* at this level is *meditation.*

49

# WORSHIP THROUGH THE STORM

Psalm 104 gives us a perfect picture of worship at both the vocal level of worship and the visual level of worship, worship that includes not only singing songs of worship but also meditating on God's Word.

*33 I will sing unto the LORD as long as I live; I will sing praise to my God while I have my being. 34 My meditation of Him shall be sweet; I will be glad in the LORD.*

**Psalm 104:33-34 (KJV)**


## THE CHOREOGRAPH LEVEL

Worship at this level involves the use of our physical body in ways that honour God. When we worship at the choreograph level we express our worship through the medium of physical action. This is the category that covers things like dancing, jumping, kneeling, bowing, prostrating, clapping, raising our hands, playing musical instruments, writing, drawing etc. This is the level at which we physically express our emotions in exaltation and appreciation of God.

*6 O come, let us worship and bow down: let us kneel before the LORD our maker. 7 For he is our God; and we are the people of his pasture, and the sheep of his hand. Today if ye will hear his voice, 8 Harden not your heart ... .*

**Psalm 95:6-8 (KJV)**

*2 Praise the LORD with harp: sing unto him with the psaltery and an instrument of ten strings. 3 Sing unto him a new song; play skilfully with a loud noise.*

**Psalm 33:2-3 (KJV)**

## THE VALUE LEVEL

Worship at this level is communicated through value. We express our worship at this level by manifesting our spiritual qualities in ways that are honouring to God. Every time we display any of God's attributes or characteristics we are expressing worship at the value level. When we operate in our God-like image, we automatically express His worth. This means that mankind functioning in his original God-like image is an expression of worship at value level. We also express God's worth by being productive, i.e. creating value, just as God does.

This is the category of worship that covers things such things as love, faith, holiness and fruitfulness – among many others.

# Worship across All Levels

We were designed by God with the capacity to worship across all four levels of worship simultaneously. The easiest way for that to happen is when we use the visual level of worship as a springboard to worship at all the other levels. This makes the expression of worship at the visual level one of the most important of all the levels of worship. Due to its ability to give direction, it forms the foundation for the expression of worship at the other levels of worship.

As humans, our whole begin tends to follow in the direction our eyes are looking and worship at the visual level has to do with what we see with our eyes. The eyes provide visual input to the whole body, and, as humans, we have both physical

# WORSHIP THROUGH THE STORM

and spiritual eyes. Here is what Jesus said concerning our eyes in Matthew 6:

*22 The lamp of the body is the eye. If therefore your eye is good, your whole body will be full of light. 23 But if your eye is bad, your whole body will be full of darkness. If therefore the light that is in you is darkness, how great is that darkness!*

**Matthew 6:22-23 (NKJV)**

With our physical eyes we see the world around us, and with our spiritual eyes we see the things of the spirit. When we worship at the visual level, using our spiritual eyes, we enthrone God in our hearts and minds by the use of our imagination. This is what enables us to easily worship God across all the other levels of worship.

Joshua was instructed by God to worship across all levels, but to start from the visual level of worship (meditation).

*8This Book of the Law shall not depart from your mouth, but you shall **meditate** in it day and night, that you may observe to do according to all that is written in it. For then you will make your way prosperous, and then you will have good success.*

**Joshua 1:8 (NKJV)**

This is why this saying is so poignant: *If you bring yourself to the place where you can see God, then you will come to truly fear and worship Him.* Worshipping across all levels brings us to the place where we are able to visualize God's promises, to see His words coming to pass in the eyes of our spirit before we actually see them with our physical eyes. With this, we can freely and easily worship God through the storm across all levels.

# Chapter 6

# Worship Is Love and

# Love Is Worship

*[29] Jesus replied, "The most important commandment is this: 'Listen, O Israel! The LORD our God is the one and only LORD. [30] And you must love the LORD your God with all your heart, all your soul, all your mind, and all your strength.' [31] The second is equally important: 'Love your neighbour as yourself.' No other commandment is greater than these."*

**– Mark 12:29-31 (NLT)**

Worship does not exist apart from love. Genuine love is worship, and genuine worship is love. Love is the highest level of worship. It is impossible to show love without the giving away of worth (worship). In the same manner, it is impossible to give worship without giving love. Worship and love are two sides of the same coin; both sides are equally important and equally needed. We demonstrate love when we truly worship, and we demonstrate worship when we truly love.

# WORSHIP THROUGH THE STORM

In Mark 12:29, when Jesus was asked what was the greatest commandment, He revealed a surprising connection between love and worship. Whilst everyone was expecting Him to at least quote the first of the twelve commandments found in Exodus 20 or say something in the line of, *"Thou shall worship the Lord thy God, and him only shalt thou serve,"* (Luke 4:8, KJV), instead He said the unexpected: *"you must love the LORD your God with all your heart, all your soul, all your mind, and all your strength."*

The depth of this statement is not apparent at first, because it seems that Jesus was making light of the Ten Commandments by relegating the most important commandment to the word *love*. In actuality, this was not the case. What He did was to summarise the essence of the whole commandment and reveal the hidden connection between love and worship. If we can bring ourselves to love God, then we can truly worship Him, because to worship is to love, and to love is to worship. Worship is love, and love is worship.

We begin to see things from a different light when we start viewing worship through the eyes of love instead of the perspective of songs and rituals. Jesus said that the entire commandment is fulfilled in just one thing: love. In other words, I can worship God by loving Him. Similarly, I can love God by worshipping Him. Here is what John the apostle said in 1 John 5:

*3 Loving God means keeping his commandments, and his commandments are not burdensome.*

**1 John 5:3 (NLT)**

Worship is expressed through love, and love is demonstrated through worship. We offer God true worship when we perfect our love for Him first and then by perfecting our love for others.

*34 A new command I give you: Love one another. As I have loved you, so you must love one another. 35 By this everyone will know that you are my disciples, if you love one another.*

**John 13:34-35**

# Chapter 7

# The Five Languages of Worship

*"It is possible to give without loving, but it is impossible to love without giving"*

**- John Wesley**

Worship is about communicating worth. It is impossible to communicate worth without giving, and giving worth in benefit of another is what constitutes love. This is essentially what worship is about.

When we truly worship, we add value to, increase the worth of and multiply the influence of the target of our worship. This is exactly the same thing that happens when we practice true love. It is then not surprising that Jesus, in Mark 12:30, could sum up God's entire commandment in one word: *love*, due to the fact that in loving God first and loving our neighbour as ourselves we are fulfilling all of His commandments.

In saying this, Jesus was also saying: provide worth to the Lord thy God first, and then provide worth to thy neighbour as you do for yourself.

# WORSHIP THROUGH THE STORM

*40 The King will reply, "Truly I tell you, whatever you did for one of the least of these brothers and sisters of mine, you did for me."*

**Matthew 25:40**

Since to love is to worship, then we can say love is synonymous with worship. It then follows that if we increase our understanding of love - how it is communicated and received - we will also automatically be increasing our understanding of worship.

We human beings were created in the exact image and likeness of God and, because of this, the way we communicate and receive love is a reflection of how God communicates and receives love. The only problem is that mankind in his fallen state can only function at his lowest possible capacity because his spirit is dead. In other words, mankind is functioning at a fraction of its potential capacity and, therefore, cannot fully reflect the image of God he was designed to portray. Even at that, we still have the dormant capacity within us to communicate and receive love in all three dimensions, i.e. body, soul and spirit.

In his book, *The Five Love Languages,* Dr. Norman Chapman, through his research and years of experience, identified five ways in which we, as human beings, are able to effectively communicate and receive love. He referred to them as love languages. He went on to list the five love languages as follows:

> ➢ Acts of Service
> ➢ Physical Touch
> ➢ Words of Affirmation
> ➢ Gifts
> ➢ Quality Time

In chapter five, we spoke about the dimensions and levels of worship. From this point on, I will interchangeably refer to these four levels of worship as worship languages.

Just as it is not enough to stop at being sincere in our expressions of love towards someone but must learn their primary love language and communicating love to them in that language, so also it is when it comes to worshipping God. Being sincere in the expression of our worship to Him is not enough. We must be willing to learn God's primary worship language and communicate our worship using that language.

## Love Languages Versus Worship Languages

The table below (*diagram 2*) contrasts the love languages with their corresponding equivalence in worship terms and the common expression they share. For example, acts of service often involve physical actions, which are the corresponding physical expression of one's favourable thoughts in honour, exultation or appreciation of the other.

| Love vs. Worship Languages | | |
|---|---|---|
| **Love** | **Worship** | **Expression** |
| Acts of Service | Choreograph / Visual | Thought |
| Physical Touch | Choreograph | Emotion |
| Words of Affirmation | Vocal | Confidence |
| Gifts | | Worth |
| Quality Time | Value | Waiting |

*Diagram 2: Love Versus Worship Languages*

# WORSHIP THROUGH THE STORM

## ACTS OF SERVICE IN WORSHIP

Acts of service speaks of recognising and doing things we know the other person is in need of and would like for us to do for them. The best example of this is seen in the life of Jacob. He was willing to serve a total of fourteen years for the hand of his wife Rachel in marriage.

*18 Jacob was in love with Rachel and said, "I'll work for you seven years in return for your younger daughter Rachel." 19 Laban said, "It's better that I give her to you than to some other man. Stay here with me." 20 So Jacob served seven years to get Rachel, but they seemed like only a few days to him because of his love for her … . I served you for Rachel, didn't I? Why have you deceived me?" 26 Laban replied, "It is not our custom here to give the younger daughter in marriage before the older one. 27 Finish this daughter's bridal week; then we will give you the younger one also, in return for another seven years of work." 28 And Jacob did so. He finished the week with Leah, and then Laban gave him his daughter Rachel to be his wife.*

**Genesis 29:18-28**

When we are in love, the burden of years of labour is lightened, making acts of service pleasurable rather than burdensome. Filled with the pleasure of favourable thoughts towards Rachel, Jacob was able to serve an additional seven years, despite having been cheated by his father-in-law.

Applying this same concept of acts of service to worship, we see that when we recognise what God is in need of and do it for Him, then we are serving Him. Many of us would think God does not have a need, but He does. The only difference is that God is the only one who can satisfy His own need. He never asks for anyone or anything in all of creation to give Him what He has not first given. So His need for worship from us is the same as His need for every part of His creation, the need for each creature to fulfil its purpose.

We were created out of God's need for something that would bring Him pleasure. Whenever we recognize this need and perform acts of service that please Him, it brings worth to Him. This is worship.

## PHYSICAL TOUCH IN WORSHIP

Physical touch speaks of physical actions that we do in response to the emotion we feel towards the one we love, as an expression of our affection towards them. When it comes to God, we can't physically touch Him in person, but we can express our favourable emotions towards Him by virtue of touching His proxy here on earth i.e., our neighbours.

We apply this concept of physical touch in worship by taking practical actions that touch and make a positive difference in the lives of our fellow human beings.

*⁴⁰ The King will reply, "Truly I tell you, whatever you did for one of the least of these brothers and sisters of mine, you did for me."*

**Matthew 25:40**

Reaching out to our fellow human beings is also reaching out to God. Touching people on His behalf is touching Him. The best example for this is illustrated in the story of the Good Samaritan, as told in Luke 10 by Jesus:

*³⁶ "Which of these three do you think was a neighbour to the man who fell into the hands of robbers?" ³⁷ The expert in the law replied, "The one who had mercy on him." Jesus told him, "Go and do likewise."*

**Luke 10:36-37**

Another way we can physically touch God by touching people is found in the book of Isaiah.

*⁶ Is not this the kind of fasting I have chosen: to loose the chains of injustice and untie the cords of the yoke, to set the oppressed free and break every yoke? ⁷ Is it not to share your food with the hungry and to provide the poor wanderer with shelter — when you see the naked, to clothe them, and not to turn away from your own flesh and blood?*

**Isaiah 58:6-7**

We can effectively judge the way we emotionally feel about God by the way we feel about other people — the crowning glory of His creation.

# WORSHIP THROUGH THE STORM

The mother or father of a child can easily tell the way a person feels towards them by the way they treat their children when no one is looking. In like manner, the true test of our love and worship of God is reflected in the way we treat His creation. All of mankind is His prized possession, the height of His creation.

## WORDS OF AFFIRMATION IN WORSHIP

Words of affirmation speaks of the kind words we say to the one we love about all their positive attributes, the words of affirmation we use to declare our admiration and confidence in their ability and characteristics. This concept can be directly applied in worship. We can directly say words about the positive attributes of God, words that affirm His ability and characteristics.

The psalmist David gives us a plethora of examples on this concept of love as it relates to worshipping God. Here is one of his psalms:

*¹ I will sing of the Lord's great love forever; with my mouth I will make your faithfulness known through all generations. ²I will declare that your love stands firm forever, that you have established your faithfulness in heaven itself.*

**Psalm 89:1-2**

In addition to singing psalms, hymns and spiritual songs, we can also put this concept of words of affirmation into practice by speaking words of edification to one another that affirm our faith in God.

*¹⁹ Speaking to one another with psalms, hymns, and songs from the Spirit. Sing and make music from your heart to the Lord.*

**Ephesians 5:19**

## THE GIVING AND RECEIVING OF GIFTS IN WORSHIP

The receiving of gifts is about the expression of our affection by way of the presenting and receiving of gifts. As the quote in the opening of this chapter says, *"It is possible to give without loving, but it is impossible to love without giving."*

The giving and receiving of gifts is universal; it is found in every human culture. God gave us the best example of this when He gave His only begotten Son for our sins, paying the full price for our redemption from sin and its consequences - death, hell, sickness and poverty. His gift to us proves how much we are worth to Him. He gave His utmost for our gravest. By receiving His gift we show that we love Him.

Jesus is God's most valuable gift to mankind. By receiving Him into our lives, we are accepting His love for us, and by giving Him the gift of our worship, we are demonstrating our love for Him.

When it comes to worship, this concept cannot be directly applied, because God is a Spirit, and therefore can't physically receive physical gifts, only spiritual ones. In light of this, the apostle Paul, in writing to the Romans, said:

*¹ Therefore, I urge you, brothers and sisters, in view of God's mercy, to offer your bodies as a living sacrifice, holy and pleasing to God — this is your true and proper worship.*

**Romans 12:1**

This does not mean God does not want us to give Him our finances and resources.

## QUALITY TIME IN WORSHIP

Quality time speaks of spending quality time in order to be in the presence of the one we love. People who are truly in love naturally have a desire to spend time with their beloved. This craving can sometimes be satisfied through no other means than the presence of the other.

This is another concept that we can directly apply in our worship. God desires for us to spend time in His presence, not just to present our petitions, but to bask in His presence and wait on Him, ready to do His bidding.

When we are truly putting this concept into practice, we are willing and ready to give and to do anything He asks of us.

# Section III

# What Is the Storm About?

# Chapter 8

# Why God Hides Treasures
# in Storms

*³ I will give you the treasures of darkness. And hidden riches of secret places,
That you may know that I, the LORD, Who call you by your name, Am the
God of Israel.*

**- Isaiah 45:3 (NKJV)**

It is the most difficult and trying times that hold life's most
valuable treasures, the darkest periods in life, times when you
can't see your right hand from your left or tell which direction
the boat of your life is heading.

God is a progressive God; therefore He provides an avenue
for everything that comes out of Him to continually increase
in value. A storm is an avenue for competition, a place of
great darkness. It provides the ultimate challenge for the
ultimate reward. The tougher the competition the more
rewarding it is for the competitor, and the more entertaining it
is for their spectators. Just as in any competition, it is always
the finals that pull in the most crowds because they provide
the highest level of competition and reward for both the
players and their audience.

# WORSHIP THROUGH THE STORM

Everyone that God has ever called has had to go through the processing of storms. Someone once said: If your life is all plain sailing, you must ask, *"God, don't You trust me enough?"* All throughout history God has used storms as a tool of refinement to increase the value of those He has chosen for a special task. Usually it is during these challenging periods that our eyes are opened, and we discover our divine assignment, God's unique plan for our lives on earth. For those who have already discovered their assignment, storms often open up new dimensions and reveal completely new layers of their assignment.

## Reasons Why God Hides Treasures in Storms

The ultimate aim of every storm is to destroy, but seeded within every storm are secret treasures, able to perform wonderful transformations in the life of whosoever finds them. As children of God, we know God will not allow what is valuable to Him to be destroyed by anything.

*⁹ For the LORD's portion is His people; Jacob is the place of His inheritance ... . He encircled him, He instructed him, He kept him as the apple of His eye. ¹¹ As an eagle stirs up its nest, Hovers over its young, Spreading out its wings, taking them up, Carrying them on its wings, ¹² So the LORD alone led him, And there was no foreign god with him.*

**Deuteronomy 32:9-12 (NKJV)**

When we are walking in and pursuing our divine purpose, storms will come, but they are never meant to sink us. Instead, they are meant to purge and refine us. When we yield to the process God is allowing the storm to take us through, the storm will then yield to us the secret treasures hidden within its deadly blow.

In the end, when the storm ceases, we will have become fully prepared and ready to walk into a new dimension, a new stage of life, endowed with the manifestation of the gifts of the Spirit of God, testifying to us and through us with signs, wonders and miracles following. We become God's proof, a testimony to our world.

There are four major reasons why God hides treasures in storms:

1. To get the best out of us
2. To help us discover our true selves
3. To prepare us for a greater task
4. To show off His splendour

## TO GET THE BEST OUT OF US

The first reason why God hides treasures in storms is that He wants to get the best out of us. He sometimes allows us to go through these seemingly unbearable challenges because He wants to get us to sparkle.

Have you ever noticed how shiny a glass looks after it has been put through a dish washer and polished? God allows storms to do the same to us, so that at the end of it all, we will sparkle with the light of His glory. God's one and only intention is to have us reflect His image here on earth.

The juice stored in a fruit can only flows out when it is squeezed. Every time we submit to God and resist the temptation of the storm to give up, we add a little more sparkle to our inner man. As we continue to follow the process and learn the lessons God want us to learn, the storm will eventually achieve the purpose of squeezing the best out of us, instead of squeezing the life out of us.

# WORSHIP THROUGH THE STORM

*[16] Therefore we do not lose heart. Even though our outward man is perishing, yet the inward man is being renewed day by day. [17] For our light affliction, which is but for a moment, is working for us a far more exceeding and eternal weight of glory.*

**2 Corinthians 4:16-17 (NKJV)**

Another way to look at it is to compare our lives to seeds. The only way the oil trapped inside a seed can be extracted is by submitting it to crushing and grinding. The oil will only flow after it is subjected to tremendous heat and pressure.

God's anointing flows freely out of us, after we have been put to the test. Storms test us, putting our character under unbelievable strain. Yet, it is this very process that releases what has been locked up within us, forcing the best to come out. So, in all, we can see that storms, though painful to endure, really bring God's best out of us.

## TO HELP US DISCOVER OUR TRUE SELVES

The second reason why God hides treasures in storms is that He wants us to discover our purpose. He gives permission to storms so that they will destroy the thing that hinders and prevents His children from fulfilling their purpose.

God has buried the seed of purpose in the heart of every man, and storms provide the most fertile soil for their germination. His highest agenda for every one of us is not that we will be comfortable and pain-free, but that we will discover our true selves.

The fulfilment of purpose is every inventor or creator's highest aim. It gives God the greatest pleasure to see us seeking Him and walking in His purpose for us. Unfortunately, fallen man, by nature, will not seek God when everything is nice and rosy, but only when things are difficult and become uncomfortable. That is when men go in search of Him.

Due to His love for us, God will allow storms to perturb our environment and cause us to look for Him and, in the process, discover His divine purpose for our lives. God sometimes allows us to go through these seemingly-unbearable challenges so that the seed of purpose He has buried within us will be discovered.

Storms expose us to our purpose. They reveal to us, often for the first time, our true selves. They allow us to see ourselves from a new perspective, beyond the blinding light of the present moment, the here and now.

Greatness is often birthed out of adversity. Sometimes we have to be unhinged from the system around us in order for us to find ourselves.

The desert experience was indispensable in preparing the children of Israel to enter the Promise Land, but it was equally instrumental in the development of Moses as one of the greatest leaders that ever lived.

*² And you shall remember that the LORD your God led you all the way these forty years in the wilderness, to humble you and test you, to know what was in your heart, whether you would keep His commandments or not.*

**Deuteronomy 8:2 (NKJV)**

As this scripture illustrates, God also leads us through wilderness situations, or storms, in order to discover the true state of our heart towards Him and to expose it to us.

In other words, storms not only expose us to our purpose; they also allow us to see the things that stand in the way of fulfilling that purpose.

Our circumstances and situations provide a platform for us to discover the greatness of our true selves. We should only allow the storm to force us to go in search of God and the discovery of His purpose for our lives.

# WORSHIP THROUGH THE STORM

The wealth of treasure hidden in storms can be found nowhere else. It is the place where purpose is discovered, refined and built. Therefore God will allow us to go through them. In the book of John it states:

*2 Every branch in Me that does not bear fruit He takes away; and every branch that bears fruit He prunes, that it may bear more fruit.*

**John 15:2 (NKJV)**

### TO PREPARE US FOR GREATER TASKS

The third reason why God hides treasures in storms is to prepare us for greater tasks. He uses storms to make us a better person and cause us to move to a place where we would not have been otherwise.

Storms are tools in God's hand, to recalibrate and equip us for our next assignment. They serve the purpose of trimming us down to the bare essentials, bringing us to the level where our sole dependence is on God, rather than our own strength, intellect, resources or connections. Storms move us to the place where we are left with no other option but trusting God and allowing Him to become our only source and only hope.

One principle by which God operates is that He will never ask anyone or anything to give what He has not first deposited into it. Before He gives anyone an assignment, He will first equip that person to fulfil that assignment because, every divine assignment requires divine assistance in order for it to be fulfilled. We cannot use a physical means to fulfil a spiritual assignment. So, in order for us to fulfil greater tasks for God, He must become our only source and only hope. And storms do that for us. They bring us to the place where our Lord becomes our Saviour and Provider.

## TO SHOW OFF HIS SPLENDOUR

The fourth reason why God hides treasures in storms is to show off His splendour.

Many of us tend to question the fact that God is glorified through our pain. What we often miss is the detail that God is not glorified *in* our pain but rather *through* our pain.

The proud mother of a newly-born child does not rejoice *in* the pain of childbearing, but she rejoices *through* it. She rejoices because of the new soul she will be bringing to experience life on earth.

She will have been waiting for nine months, expectantly looking forward to the delivery day, not because she relishes the pain, but rather what will result *from* the pain.

God wants to bring to life His glory through our lives, and often times this process is very painful. Jesus had to go through pain and suffering in order to give birth to God's plan of redemption for sinful man. Now mankind can once again show off God's splendour, but only because of what Jesus had to endure on the cross.

*² Fixing our eyes on Jesus, the pioneer and perfecter of faith. For the joy set before him he endured the cross, scorning its shame, and sat down at the right hand of the throne of God.*

**Hebrews 12:2**

In like manner, God will allow us to go through the storms of life so that we can give birth to His splendour. When we follow the process and learn the lessons, it will always result in the display of His glory in and through our lives. This is how we become beacons of light and pinches of salt to our generation, showing off the glory and splendour of our heavenly Father.

# Chapter 9

# Your Power Is in Your Pain

*"All of God's promise will meet you at your place of greatest pain"*
## - Bishop T.D. Jakes

## Why God does not intervene in our Crisis

God allows pain so we can use the power to fulfil purpose. If He cushions us from every blow or keeps us away from every storm, we won't grow.

Some of life's greatest lessons are taught in the stormy seasons of life. The reason a good teacher will allow his student to go through an exam and not interfere with the process is the same one why God allows us to go through storms without intervening. Consider this passage in the book of Proverbs:

*¹⁰ If you falter in a time of trouble, how small is your strength!*
**Proverbs 24:10**

There is power to be tapped in the treasury of pain. A butterfly will forever remain a caterpillar if it fails to move into its most painful season of life - the chrysalis stage of development. Anything that interferes with this process truncates or hinders its entire development.

Without the chrysalis stage, the caterpillar will still have the potential of a butterfly, but will not have the ability to become one. It will have a dream to become beautiful and be able to fly, but it will be stuck with the reality of perpetually being at the same stage of development. It will be trapped by its unwillingness to go through the pain that would give birth to the next season of life - butterfly season - a season of beauty, abundance and flight.

Side-stepping the chrysalis stage of development would also be side-stepping the period of greatest growth, the most challenging stage in which potential develops into ability.

It is through pain that potential is transformed into ability. Avoiding the pain of the transformation process is to also avoid the release of the power stored up in it.

The storms of life can be compared to the chrysalis stage of development in the life of a butterfly. The butterfly starts its life as an egg. The egg hatches into a creepy, crawly caterpillar with a voracious appetite. It is hatched among lush green foliage, an abundant source and supply of food from which to feed on to its hearts content. This remains the case for a period of time, but then he storm hits.

Growing up in a tropical climate with lots of foliage around, I was privilege to have observed the development of butterflies. When it was their season, the mothers would lay their eggs only on particular trees - not just any tree. Some fruit trees have sweet leaves, compared to other trees. The trees butterflies pick are usually large fruits trees with thick, lush green foliage.

The little caterpillars are birthed on these green pastures, a place where they can eat and continue to eat to their satisfaction. They will keep growing and putting on more and more weight as a result.

Within a couple of weeks that huge tree with lovely green foliage will become bare, stripped of all its leaves, like a tree in autumn. These voracious eating machines will have devoured every single leaf on the great tree, and this once green pasture has now become a horrid-looking, bone-dry desert of bark. All the vegetation is gone, all the foliage completely disappeared.

The caterpillars are now left with nothing to eat and nowhere else to find food. Thus begins their new stage of development, the start of their season of storm.

Some of them will slip and fall off the tree because there are no more leaves to squirm on. The branch and stem of the tree is hard to cling to, and their forage has become a dry desert of hard tree bark.

Due to the weight they have put on in the last season, the first challenge for the caterpillars now becomes learning how to maintain their balance in order to be able to move around without falling off. Their movement drastically slows down, as they learn how to navigate around their new environment. Any careless move - as in the previous season - will result in a loss of balance, sending them crashing to the ground.

This is usually a terrible sight to behold. The once beautiful fruit tree now looks barren and scary, with creepy-crawlies littered round about it. Those caterpillars that have fallen off are frantically moving about looking for a safe spot, a refuge or sanctuary, whilst the others move around scavenging for food.

Can you imagine the impression chewing the bitter tree bark leaves on their tiny taste buds? It is a lingering bad taste that they will have to put up with. Then, the bitterness slowly subsides and fades away. This is what caterpillars are feeling at this stage in their development process. Our season of storms can leave us with the same bitter impression in our minds, but we should always protect our focus by keeping our mind on the end result.

*12 Not that I have already obtained all this, or have already arrived at my goal, but I press on to take hold of that for which Christ Jesus took hold of me. 13 Brothers and sisters, I do not consider myself yet to have taken hold of it. But one thing I do: Forgetting what is behind and straining toward what is ahead, 14 I press on toward the goal to win the prize for which God has called me heavenward in Christ Jesus.*

**Philippians 3:12-14**

Returning to the idea of the metamorphosis of caterpillars: in another couple of weeks, with no more food to eat, these eating machines gradually run out of energy and become immobile. As they do so, their skin starts to thicken. Within a week, the heat of the sun and the lack of food will cause their skins to thicken so much so that they become rather solid, forming a pupa. This is the stage when the old structure starts to disintegrate, and the new structure starts forming.

This process takes a couple of weeks, and after this metamorphosis is complete, the once hardened skin becomes as brittle as an egg shell.

However like a chick pecking its way out of its shell, that once ugly-looking caterpillar undergoes a marvellous transformation. A newly-formed creature gradually pecks its way out of its shell. Its figure and characteristics are diametrically opposed to its former self. It emerges with a well-rounded body, beautifully shaped wings, slick long legs and splendid colours, complete with fanciful antennas.

What a beautiful sight to behold! And what a contrasting transformation! Passing seasons have brought this about, the season of abundance, in which everything was there, ready and available, followed by the season of bareness and struggle. Afterwards came the period of yielding and waiting, which led to the final stage, a stage of transformation and maturation.

In order to fully understand why our power is in our pain, we have to understand that the process of metamorphosis in the life of a butterfly is no different from the developmental stages in the life of a child of God. A season of available abundance is followed by one of storm, and then bareness and struggle, and yet the final stage is the place of total dependence, where transformation and maturation happens. This is our sabbatical period, when we learn to rest in God and to wait on Him. In this stage, we develop our muscle of faith, trusting in every one of His words and promises.

When we rest in God, we exhibit our confidence in Him. In other words, we express worship in the value level. This period of resting in God culminates in the release of a power from within us that breaks down the "old you," replacing it with the "new you." The result is a beautiful sight to behold, the old marvellously transformed into the new.

## Lessons from the Caterpillar

God has provided a miracle, a daily provision, for each of us. It may be different from what we had in the previous season or stage of life. Nonetheless, during the storm, what we possess is exactly what we will need for that particular stage of life.

At this stage of life, when you ask God for daily bread, as His Word promises, He will answer. He will provide, but it is not the bread of the previous season, the kind you are used to feeding on. The temptation is to approach every new season with an appetite for last season's food. Jesus knew this very well and was able to effectively ward off the temptation to crave for yesterday's bread to satisfy today's hunger.

*4 Jesus answered, "It is written: 'Man shall not live on bread alone, but on every word that comes from the mouth of God.' "*

**Matthew 4:4 (NKJV)**

Most times, in the thick of the storm, our food runs out, and we find it an impossible task to support our appetite. The baggage of responsibilities gradually starts weighing us down, slowly grinding us to a halt. We call out to God, but it seems He is not hearing us. Nothing in our situation or circumstance seems to be changing for the better, so we begin to think God has abandoned us, that He is not with us. We feel we are left to pace frantically about in the barrenness of the place we find ourselves. There seems to be no respite, no time to relax or rest and enjoy the necessities of life, as was the case in the previous season. We become defenceless, exposed and at the mercy of hostile and predatory creatures.

As we struggle to scrape out a living some slip and fall under the pressure of their own weight. They fall off the very tree that has been their source of supply and shelter. Then, just like the caterpillar, they start hysterically running about, searching for food and shelter in all the wrong places and sampling everything they can find. Unfortunately, nothing tastes the same as before; they fill the stomach but lack the ability to satisfy. This was the same thing that happened after the children of Israel had crossed the Red Sea.

*5 We remember the fish we ate in Egypt at no cost — also the cucumbers, melons, leeks, onions and garlic. 6 But now we have lost our appetite; we never see anything but this manna!*

**Numbers 11:5-6**

The supply has run out, but with the appetite of yesterday still driving us on, we go in search of relief from the storm. However, nothing seems to work. Slowly but surely we start grinding to a halt, immobilised by the depletion of our reserves and lack of solution to provide for our everyday needs. The basic needs of yesterday now look like an unattainable luxury. What was once readily available and easily attainable now seems impossible.

At this stage, as we fully surrender to the workings and purpose of the storm God has allowed in our lives, our transformation into the new stage of life, our metamorphosis, begins. God starts renewing our appetite, restructuring our shape, reforming our character and beautifying us. Emotionally it feels contrary, compared to what is actually taking place, but the opposite is true.

We feel crushing pains from every angle, pains of being hungry, vulnerable, fearful and lonely. Yet, this time is our finest moment. It is getting us ready for a new season of life, a new level and dimension of functionality and operation. No longer will we be creeping and crawling among leaves and stuck just on one tree; we will be free to soar on wings and fly, liberated to hop onto and feast on as many fruit trees as we desire. Oh what a freedom!

The whole process of metamorphosis is not only to transform the caterpillar into a beautiful butterfly and give it freedom and pleasure, but to also give it the capacity to become fruitful, equipped to reproduce its own kind.

So, your power is really and truly embedded in your pain. The pain of the storm you are going through is waiting to release in you an awesome power, as you learn to depend on God and worship Him.

# Chapter 10

# At Peace through the Storm

*37 And there arose a great storm of wind, and the waves beat into the ship, so that it was now full. 38 And he was in the hinder part of the ship, asleep on a pillow: and they awake him, and say unto him, Master, carest thou not that we perish?*

**- Mark 4:37-38 (KJV)**

Jesus was at peace, so much so that He was deep in sleep, even as the storm raged around Him. His rest, however, was interrupted by the anxiety the twelve disciples felt, fearful that they were going to perish in the sea. Their despair drove them to levy an accusation of neglect on Jesus, crying out: *"Master, care ye not that we perish?"*

I don't know about you, but there have been times when I have asked a similar question, *"Father, care Ye not that I perish? Save me from the vengeance of this storm that is threatening my life!"* This is especially so when we have prayed, cried, planned and acted in faith, and yet we find ourselves still in the same situation, stuck in the same position, and seemingly going nowhere.

Due to the fact that a good number of the disciples were experienced fishermen, I want to believe they would have deployed their expertise to try and steer clear of the storm and stabilize the boat. However, the use of their strength and expert knowledge was rendered powerless by the magnitude of the storm they were up against.

I can imagine Peter, the expert fisherman, now head sailor, standing at the bow of the boat and shouting out orders to the other disciples. Matthew, the customs officer, and Thomas, the doubter, would have been terrifyingly holding on to the side of the boat, looking on and hoping this saga would soon end. Peter would have given out orders such as, "James, pull down the sail."

James might have responded, "We have tried it; it's not working."

I imagine Peter shouting back, "Lighten the load; throw some cargo overboard."

And James may have shouted back, "It is not working!"

Having tried all they knew to do and found that nothing was working, Peter, noticing the next big wave coming, would no doubt have shouted out to the rest, "Hold on tight!" But before they could gain a tight grip, another wave would hit the boat, knocking everyone off their feet.

Now Thomas was convinced they were going to drown. Grabbing Jesus's shoulder and vigorously shaking Him, He would have cried out at the top of his lungs in desperation: *"Master, are You still sleeping? Carest thou not that we perish?"*

Jesus was always at peace, and He remained at peace that day because He knew that nothing could stop Him when pursuing His divine purpose. He was confident no force was big enough to hinder Him when He was at the centre of His Father's will.

Sometimes storms come to awaken us into our purpose and to test our resolve in pursuing our God-ordained mission on earth. Storms awaken us and set us on the path of exploring God's plan for our lives. In the case in which we have not yet come to the knowledge and full understanding of the purpose for our existence, storms provide a compelling reason for us to discover why we are who we are and why we are where we are.

The greatest benefit of storms is their ability to condition our minds to venture out into new areas and to take the risk of fully trusting God with our entire life. Consequently, temporary pains inflicted on us by the storm turns out to work for our good.

*[17] For our light affliction, which is but for a moment, is working for us a far more exceeding and eternal weight of glory.*

**2 Corinthians 4:17 (KJV)**


## Growing Up in the Face of Challenge

There are certain things we cannot escape from or pray our way out of because they are part of the growing-up process, and we must go through them. For instance, there's the hurt and pain of teething while growing a new tooth.

*[33] These things I have spoken to you, that in Me you may have peace. In the world you will have tribulation; but be of good cheer, I have overcome the world.*

**John 16:33 (KJV)**

Storms are part of the Christian growth process. My interpretation of the above passage would be: *"Bad things happen to good people, so cheer up; it's just life."* In a nutshell, "Be at peace. Get on and get ahead with your life, in spite of whatever storm you may be facing.

If you will take the time to look back on your life, you will be amazed to see things God has said to you that you have swept under the carpet, things that may now mean everything

# WORSHIP THROUGH THE STORM

about where you currently find yourself and where He is taking you.

When storms come, have you noticed how the trees sway in the direction of the wind? Every time they do so, they strengthen their roots. These winds force them to grow deeper and spread wider, thus increasing their hold on the soil. In the same way, storms strengthen us and cause us to be enlarged. Storms constrain us to venture out into new territories, thereby increasing our productivity.

Overcoming storms causes us to yield the result of increased fruitfulness, when we have learned to be at peace through the storm. Like Jesus, we have to come to the place that we have full assurance that nothing can stop or hinder us when we are pursuing God's purpose for our lives. When this happens, we can boldly say, *"No matter what, I will be at peace through the storm.'*

The storms of life will blow, and the devil may throw all his deadly arsenal at me, but my heart is steadfast and my mind resolute. Like Jesus, I will sleep. I choose to be at peace through the storm, confidently resting in the arms of the One whose purpose I am on earth to accomplish.

# Section IV

# Worshipping through the Storm

# Chapter 11

# Tapping into the Treasures

# Hidden in the Storm

*[28] And we know that in all things God works for the good of those who love him, who have been called according to his purpose.*

### - Romans 8:28 (NIV)

God is a generous God; He wants us to experience His miraculous provision every day and at every stage of our lives. For this reason, He hides treasure in the most unusual of places - in a storm. Our challenge, therefore, is to discover these hidden treasures and to tap into the provision God has made available to us for this particular period of our life.

Seizing the opportunity to discover and tap into the treasures hidden within the storm will require our full confidence in the knowledge that by allowing us to go through the storm, God is ultimately working things out for our good. This certainly calls for a new set of lenses, a different perspective for looking at our circumstance.

One of that set of lenses is called *faith*. Faith will accustom our mind to the truth that *there is a miracle in every storm.*

# WORSHIP THROUGH THE STORM

Another set of lenses that gives us a fresh perspective that will enable us to discern the treasures hidden in the storm is putting on an attitude of thankfulness.

*18 In everything give thanks; for this is the will of God in Christ Jesus for you.*

**1 Thessalonians 5:18 (NKJV)**

An attitude of thanksgiving sharpens our sensitivity and positions us to take advantage of the treasures in the storm. It switches on the perspective of faith by penetrating the dark clouds of doubt that characterises the storm. In other words, it moves us from fear, grumbling and complaining, to faith, peace and joy.

We have to be able to appreciate and submit to the process God is allowing the storm to take us through. When we do, the process develops our faith in God, allowing us to remain confident and trusting that everything we are going through will ultimately work out for our good. This is what causes our faith to grow. A change of perspective will always result in a change in our ability to tap into treasures once hidden.

The best example of this is seen in Matthew 14:

*28 And Peter answered Him and said, "Lord, if it is You, command me to come to You on the water." 29 So He said, "Come." And when Peter had come down out of the boat, he walked on the water to go to Jesus. 30 But when he saw that the wind was boisterous, he was afraid; and beginning to sink he cried out, saying, "Lord, save me!" 31 And immediately Jesus stretched out His hand and caught him, and said to him, "O you of little faith, why did you doubt?"*

**Matthew 14:28-31 (NKJV)**

Peter was able to confidently step out of the boat and consequently walked on water. It was his perspective that enabled him to walk on the water; his perspective kept him afloat. But the moment his focus moved away from Jesus, he began to sink. He started drowning, not because he lost faith or no longer trusted the words of Jesus, but because his perspective had changed. The instant he turned his face away from Jesus, his perspective changed. When his perspective changed, his focus also changed and, as a result, he placed more worth on the storm than he did on Jesus at that very instant.

Before he stepped out of the boat Peter must have said to himself, "This is Jesus; I can trust His word." But he began to sink the moment his perspective changed, because he was now saying to himself, "Hey, if this figure turns out to be a ghost and not Jesus, what options do I have to save myself? How far am I from the boat?"

## Keys to Tapping into the Treasures Hidden in the Storm

Faith and thanksgiving help us to locate the treasure chest in the storm, but we need the keys in order to tap into that chest. There are keys that each of us who is going through a stormy season of life can use to open up the treasure chest of the storm and cause it to yield its bountiful treasures to us. However, like any key, these are useless unless they are used. The treasure trough of the storm has a combination lock that will require the use of three keys to uncover the secret treasures they contain. The keys are found in the three major principles listed below:

1. *Look beyond the challenge.*

2. *Pray and ask God for daily bread.*

3. *Spend the best part of your time worshipping God.*

### LOOK BEYOND THE CHALLENGE

This is the first key to tapping into the treasures hidden in the storm. This key opens up the outer compartment of the storm's treasure chest, by allowing us to look beyond the present challenge.

Doing this switches our perspective and focus away from the pain to the result that the pain will eventually give birth to. We must start seeing the destination God has prepared for us and the purpose He is equipping us to fulfil.

*⁹ However, as it is written: "What no eye has seen, what no ear has heard, and what no human mind has conceived" — the things God has prepared for those who love him."*

**1 Corinthians 2:9**


## PRAY AND ASK GOD FOR DAILY BREAD

This is the second key to tapping into the treasures hidden in the storm. This key opens up the middle compartment of the treasure chest, by allowing us to communicate directly with the Master of the treasure.

*⁹ In this manner, therefore, pray: Our Father in heaven, Hallowed be Your name. ¹⁰ Your kingdom come. Your will be done on earth as it is in heaven. ¹¹ Give us this day our daily bread.*

**Matthew 6:9-11 (NKJV)**

During periods of storm, daily bread speaks of something more than just food for the belly. Jesus, in Matthew 4:4, said: *"Man shall not live by bread alone but by every word that proceeds out of the mouth of God"* (Version?).

There are things that will not be given to us until we ask for them, treasures that will otherwise remain hidden until we ask God to reveal them to us. That is why, even in the midst of the storm, we must pray and ask God to give us our daily bread, revelation that will sustain us through the storm.

For us to fully tap into the treasures in the storm, we have to get to the place where, like Jesus, we will say:

# Tapping into the Treasures Hidden in the Storm

*³⁴ My food is to do the will of Him who sent Me, and to finish His work.*
**John 4:34 (NKJV)**

## SPEND THE BEST PART OF YOUR TIME WORSHIPPING GOD

This is the third and final key to tapping into the treasures hidden in the storm. Worship is the key that opens up the innermost compartment of the treasure chest. It unlocks the door of God's presence, granting us free access to signs, wonders and miracles.

Worship is the reason for which mankind was created, and by worshipping God we fulfil our purpose. Because of this, it then becomes impossible for us to not also attract the approval and support of God, when we offer Him true worship.

As discussed in chapter three, *"The Meaning of True Worship,"* worship goes way beyond the singing of songs and the performance of rituals. Worship is about doing that which brings worth to God.

It is God's approval that unveils the secret riches stored up in the storm, and these hidden treasures only give up their secrets through worship. Therefore it is only wise that, after changing our perspective and putting on the lenses of thankfulness and faith, we also should put on the garment of thanksgiving, by spending the rest and best of our time worshipping God.

My mother told me of a time when she was in a stormy situation, facing a big challenge. She was outdoors walking across a field and praying about this issue, when God spoke to her and said, "Look up at the sky. Can you see the beginning and the end of it? As small as you look, compared to the expanse of the sky, so also are your problems to Me. When

# WORSHIP THROUGH THE STORM

you focus on Me, I am magnified. So also, when you focus on the problem, it becomes magnified in your eye."

This same word applies to us whenever we find ourselves in the middle of a stormy situation. We have to look up to heaven and focus on God. Give Him your worship in the midst of our challenges. When He is magnified, every other thing becomes small and insignificant.

As we spend time worshipping God, the present moment gradually fades into obscurity. The challenges lose their grip on us, as we start seeing the storm from another dimension. Everything pales into insignificance, as we look at things from God's perspective. Thus, we are able to tap into every treasure hidden in the storm for us.

# Chapter 12

# The Weapon of Worship

*[21] ... Jehoshaphat appointed men to sing to the LORD and to praise him for the splendour of his holiness as they went out at the head of the army, saying: "Give thanks to the LORD, for his love endures forever." [22] As they began to sing and praise, the LORD set ambushes against the men of Ammon and Moab and Mount Seir who were invading Judah, and they were defeated."*

**- 2 Chronicles 20:21-22**

Worship is man's most valuable possession. It is the most powerful weapon available to mankind on earth. We have victory through worship.

Worship has turned the hearts of kings, reversed the decrees of cruel dictators and broken the shackles off of prisoners, releasing them from captivity. It has brought down unconquerable walls and rendered helpless the might of the strong.

Worship has transformed the lives of slave girls into queens who rule over empires. The notoriety of prostitutes and thieves has been transformed and perpetuated into a legacy of royalty through worship. Worship has taken a shepherd boy, made him the talk of the town, and enthroned him as king over an entire nation.

# WORSHIP THROUGH THE STORM

Confronting superior military might with drums, trumpets, singers and dancers is one of the most ridiculous strategies you could ever come up with to face a more powerful military foe. Yet, one of the most inspiring military victories of all time came from using this very strategy. The courage to deploy the weapon of worship against the enemy may appear to be ridiculous, but it is an effective strategy. Worship is capable of wrecking the mind of the opposing army.

When King Jehoshaphat employed this strategic weapon of worship against a larger and much more sophisticated army, his resulting victory left a mark in the history of warfare.

*21 After consulting the people, Jehoshaphat appointed men to sing to the LORD and to praise Him for the splendour of His holiness as they went out at the head of the army, saying: "Give thanks to the LORD, for His love endures forever." 22 As they began to sing and praise, the LORD set ambushes against the men of Ammon and Moab and Mount Seir who were invading Judah, and they were defeated. 23 The Ammonites and Moabites rose up against the men from Mount Seir to destroy and annihilate them. After they finished slaughtering the men from Seir, they helped to destroy one another. 24 When the men of Judah came to the place that overlooks the desert and looked toward the vast army, they saw only dead bodies lying on the ground; no one had escaped.*

**2 Chronicles 20:21-24**

The "element of surprise" was so intense here that it literally caused a nervous convulsion, a powerful shockwave to the nervous system of the opposing army. This sparked off a barrage of friendly fire, each soldier turning against the other. It was pandemonium, confusion at its highest and deadliest degree.

That day Israel defeated a much more formidable and superior army without a sword in hand, but with the praises of God on their lips. They chose to engage the weapon of worship, honouring God's word above the dictates of the prevailing situation and circumstance. In this way, they obtained their victory through worship.

# A Weapon of Spiritual Warfare

Worship is the most powerful weapon available to the New Testament believer, and so the highest level of spiritual warfare is fought over the ownership of our worship. God is the rightful owner of the worship of all of creation, because He created everything. The devil's one and only aim has been to subvert the worship of mankind - God's most precious creation. Therefore he puts up his fiercest fight to achieve this goal. Forearmed with this knowledge, we can thwart all of his strategies and trample underfoot all of his efforts.

By worshipping God we are directly using the weapon of worship against the devil. When we worship God, we strip the devil of his influence over our terrestrial body. Worshipping God reconnects the spirit within us with its Source, and when this happens, it releases a tremendous power that catapults us into the consciousness of the spirit. We begin to experience God's presence, and wonderful changes start taking place within and around us. We receive answers to prayers; things that were once impossible suddenly become possible. God seems to now respond to every one of our requests.

The measure to which we worship God is the measure to which He is revealed to us. The dimension and level of God's glory we can access is in direct correlation to the dimension and level we truly worship Him.

In the Old Testament, when Joshua was confronted with the seemingly impenetrable walls of Jericho, God asked Him to employ the weapon of worship.

*2 Then the LORD said to Joshua, "See, I have delivered Jericho into your hands, along with its king and its fighting men. 3 March around the city once with all the armed men. Do this for six days. 4 Have seven priests carry trumpets of rams' horns in front of the ark. On the seventh day, march around the city seven times, with the priests blowing the trumpets. 5 When you hear them sound a long blast on the*

# WORSHIP THROUGH THE STORM

*trumpets, have the whole army give a loud shout; then the wall of the city will collapse and the army will go up, everyone straight in ... .²⁰ When the trumpets sounded, the army shouted, and at the sound of the trumpet, when the men gave a loud shout, the wall collapsed; so everyone charged straight in, and they took the city.*

**Joshua 6:2-20**

## Worship While You Wait

Worship is the fastest way out of any storm, however remember, the fastest way does not necessarily mean the shortest way. Worship takes you into God's presence, where there is no impossibility. What this then means is that our breaking through and coming out of the storm is dependent upon us worshipping while we wait.

This season of storm won't last. Just as the pain of childbirth does not last forever, so also the pain of the storm we may be experiencing. These pains are a sign that we are in the process of giving birth to something new - a new season of prosperity and greatness on every side. In the meantime, let us turn our face towards heaven, fix our focus on God and give Him the utmost of our worship. The miracles that will result will speak for themselves, as proof of our faith in Him.

# Chapter 13

# A Spiritual Currency

*Worship is the currency of God's Kingdom.*

Man was made for worship; our very existence is worship. Worship can't be stopped; it can only be perverted or misdirected. Worship is an indelible part of our functionality as human beings. God created us in such a way that the act of just being alive is worship in and of itself. This means mankind - so long as there is breath in him - is incapable of stopping himself from giving worship. We can never get ourselves to the place where we become dormant or neutral worshippers, except at death.

What all of this implies is that, at any given moment, we are consciously or subconsciously worshipping someone or something. The decisions of our hearts and the subsequent actions they produce attribute our worship to either God or the devil.

*[16] Don't you know that when you offer yourselves to someone as obedient slaves, you are slaves of the one you obey — whether you are slaves to sin, which leads to death, or to obedience, which leads to righteousness? [17] But thanks be to God that, though you used to be slaves to sin, you have come to obey from your heart the pattern of teaching that has now claimed your allegiance.*

**Romans 6:16-17**

# WORSHIP THROUGH THE STORM

From the above passage we can see that whoever we decide to obey gains ownership of our worship. They become the owner of everything that belongs to us, which includes our worship.

Further on in this same passage, the apostle Paul lays out the reason why we must consciously choose to worship God.

*¹ Therefore, I urge you, brothers and sisters, in view of God's mercy, to offer your bodies as a living sacrifice, holy and pleasing to God — this is your true and proper worship. ² Do not conform to the pattern of this world, but be transformed by the renewing of your mind. Then you will be able to test and approve what God's will is — his good, pleasing and perfect will.*

**Romans 12:1-2**

## The Spiritual Currency of God's Kingdom

Worship is a spiritual currency; it is the currency by which God's kingdom operates. Worship is man's most valuable possession. It can never be given without provoking a response; it is never traded for nothing.

Genuine heartfelt and sincere worship is of much weight and value; so much so that no recipient of it, whether man or spiritual being, can afford to stay unperturbed at its receipt. Thus, worship has never been given without resulting in an equal or greater measure in response to the worship given. The measure of the response is usually commensurate to the magnitude and magnificence of the recipient of such worship.

A little girl worshipped a king through dancing, and he offered her as much as half of his kingdom.

*²² And when the daughter of the said Herodias came in, and danced, and pleased Herod and them that sat with him, the king said unto the damsel, Ask of me whatsoever thou wilt, and I will give it thee. ²³ And he sware unto her, Whatsoever thou shalt ask of me, I will give it thee, unto the half of my kingdom.*

## Mark 6:22-23 (KJV)

If a wicked king can give such an outrageous gift, because of receiving a worship that pleased him, then can you imagine what God - the Creator of all things - will do for the worshipper who pleases Him?

*⁹ But as it is written, Eye hath not seen, nor ear heard, neither have entered into the heart of man, the things which God hath prepared for them that love [**worship**] him.*

## 1 Corinthians 2:9 (KJV)

Worship is a two-way street. When we truly worship God, He rewards us by revealing more of Himself to us. The reward of His presence far outweighs what we are presently capable of handling or understand. Wherever God's presence is made manifest there is no impossibility. His presence causes the limitations of time, space and matter to disappear.

The spiritual currency of worship is the only thing we can trade for God's presence. No amount of wisdom, money, fame or power can reward us with His presence. Worship is the spiritual currency required for transacting in God's presence.

God's presence reveals His glory. Our prayer will reveal His acts to us, but our worship will reveal His heart. The legal principle of prayer will give us access to His gifts, but the spiritual principle of worship will give us access to His presence. When His heart is revealed to us, we see His glory, and when we reveal our own heart to Him, we start to see signs, miracles and wonders taking place within and around us.

# WORSHIP THROUGH THE STORM

*17 And these signs will accompany those who believe: In my name they will drive out demons; they will speak in new tongues.*

**Mark 16:17**

## TRANSACTING IN THE SPIRITUAL CURRENCY OF WORSHIP

The Bible is full of stories of people who did transactions using the spiritual currency of worship and received the desires of their heart. When Jesus walked the face of the earth, everyone who came to Him using this spiritual currency received in return their heart's desire.

*2 And, behold, there came a leper and worshipped him, saying, Lord, if thou wilt, thou canst make me clean. 3 And Jesus put forth his hand, and touched him, saying, I will; be thou clean. And immediately his leprosy was cleansed.*

**Matthew 8:2-3 (KJV)**

God's presence is at work today in our generation, changing the estate of those who have discovered and employed the use of the spiritual currency of true worship. Healing, deliverance and the dead literally coming back to life are some of the notable proofs of how men and women of our time have accessed God's heart through worship. They have knocked down the doors of impossibilities within and around them. They have unlocked the door of God's presence by transacting in the spiritual currency of worship.

Each of us can do the same, by starting to consciously use the spiritual currency of worship in our spiritual transactions with heaven. God has already provided all that we may ever be in need of, but we can only gain full access to them by transacting in the spiritual currency of true worship.

*[3] His divine power has given us everything we need for a godly life through our knowledge of him who called us by his own glory and goodness.*

**2 Peter 1:3**

# Section V

# The Conclusion

# Chapter 14

# Worship through the Storm

*¹ Sing, barren woman, you who never bore a child; burst into song, shout for joy, you who were never in labour; because more are the children of the desolate woman than of her who has a husband," says the LORD.*

## - Isaiah 54:1

When God is onboard the boat of our lives, there is no challenge that is big enough to stop us, no storm powerful enough to sink our boat. God trusts us enough to allow us to go through the storm. He has confidence in the ability He has deposited inside every one of us to express His dominion here on earth. The irony is that even though God is very much interested in sailing onboard our boat, the only way He can be kept onboard is through worship. By giving God the worship that is due to Him we are not only fulfilling His purpose for our lives; we are also safeguarding the power within us to rise above any storm.

In life, there are many things that the devil throws against us to compete for our worship - the deadliest of these being storms. The good news is that when we have God onboard our boat, storms can only serve one purpose: to bring us to the place where our worship is between God Himself and us.

As believers, the outcome of every storm is ultimately working for our good. God is saying to us, as believers in the twenty-first century, the same thing He said, through the apostle Paul, to the first century believers in Rome: *"Every storm will work for your good."* It may not feel like that when we are going through it, but that is the truth.

*28 And we know that all things work together for good to those who love God, to those who are the called according to His purpose*

**Romans 8:28**

Storms are an integral part of life on earth. We know they will come, but oftentimes they hit when we least expect them and in the areas where we are least prepared. Here is what Jesus Himself said in the book of John:

*33 "I have told you these things, so that in me you may have peace. In this world you will have trouble. But take heart! I have overcome the world."*

**John 16:33**

## You can Worship through Your Storm

Worshiping God through the storm requires faith, and storms are the testing ground for real faith. Storms are the best determinant of the measure of your faith. You can only know the level of your faith by the level or category of storm it is able to survive.

If the worst thing you can ever imagine happens to you, and, like Job, you have searched your heart and found no fault within you, would you be able to still stand in the midst of the storm and say, *"Though he slay me, yet will I trust him"* (**Job 13:15, KJV**)?

In Job's case, his wife's suggested solution is symbolic of those who lose the little faith they have in the midst of a storm. They are those who really don't have a strong personal relationship with God or possibly don't even really know Him. Because their spiritual strength is small, when they find themselves in a storm, they choose the seemingly easy way out, by switching from faith to natural logic. They choose to compromise their belief instead of holding on; they go for the option of lowering their standards and values, in order to have a reprieve from the pain inflicted by the storm. Here is what Job's wife said:

*⁹ Then his wife said to him, "Do you still hold fast to your integrity? Curse God and die!"*

**Job 2:9 (NKJV)**

In contrast, there are numerous examples of other people in the Bible - in addition to Job - who chose to hold on to their faith and worship God through the storm, people like Paul and Silas, who, despite the pain and agony of being beaten, shackled and locked up in prison, demonstrated their faith by worshipping God through their ordeal. Another person was Stephen, who worshipped through the storm by demonstrating love. He was the one who, instead of praying for God's judgement to come upon the people who were persecuting him, chose to pray that God would forgive them (see Acts 7). In praying for the forgiveness of his persecutors, Stephen expressed worship at its highest level and, in the midst of the storm, experienced God's presence.

*⁵⁸ And they cast him out of the city and stoned him. And the witnesses laid down their clothes at the feet of a young man named Saul. ⁵⁹ And they stoned Stephen as he was calling on God and saying, "Lord Jesus, receive my spirit." ⁶⁰ Then he knelt down and cried out with a loud voice, "Lord, do not charge them with this sin." And when he had said this, he fell asleep.*

**Acts 7:58-60 (NKJV)**

# WORSHIP THROUGH THE STORM

There are other biblical examples of people who worshipped through the storm, people who persevered through pain, enduring severe hardship and yet worshipping. By their unwavering faith in God, they expressed their worship of Him through the storm. This includes people like David, Peter, John, and even Jesus Christ, our Lord and Saviour.

We can and must worship God through the storm. When we worship Him through the storm it proves that the faith we have is real. The storm is the place where we can give our utmost for His utmost, our highest level of worship for His highest level of reward.

## Encountering the Power of Worship

Revelation is the fuel for worship. The moment we become aware and are able to develop the mind-set of seeing storms as the breeding ground for a higher calling - our divine purpose - then a new confidence is birthed within us. This is the confidence that will cause us to worship and to be at peace in the eye of the storm, in the same way Jesus was sound asleep in the middle of a storm. This confidence is an expression of worship at the value level.

Worship will take us to a position in God to which simple prayer cannot get us. When we pray, God answers by revealing His acts, but when we worship, He reveals His ways to us. Worship empowers us to stand in a position where we can encounter God's power. We can only get to the place where the storms will obey our command in prayer when we have an encounter with the power released through worship.

We may see no reason to worship because of the graveness of the situation in which we find ourselves. However, we should always be cognisant of the truth that our victory is really and truly embedded in our worship. It is in these situations and circumstances that we have to learn to depend on the Holy Spirit's help.

We should ask for the grace of God to help us to offer up our most valuable asset of worship unto God. The Holy Spirit is God's enabling power, His grace. He is not only able to assist us in worshipping through the storm; He is also able to strengthen us during the waiting period.

*[16] Let us then approach God's throne of grace with confidence, so that we may receive mercy and find grace to help us in our time of need.*

**Hebrews 4:16**

I heard a story about a group of university students in Africa who found themselves still on campus at the end of the term, hoping to find a summer job placement in the city. They had run out of money and run out of food. After fruitlessly spending several hours dwelling on their situation, they were convinced that it was hopeless. And nothing was going to improve the situation any time soon, since their parents were so far away, and they did not know anyone in that vicinity who might be of help.

It was at this point that the realization suddenly dawned on one of them that their thinking and worrying over the situation would not change anything. He decided to switch over to worship. Snapped out of the prevailing mood of doom and gloom and moving into a mode of rejoicing, he started singing joyful songs of praise and, in this way, worshipping God. Then an idea came to him to go out and seek an appointment in one of the local business offices. He decided to leave his friends on campus and go into the city. The friends were bewildered by his upbeat mood and started making sarcastic comments, comments such as: *"Make sure you don't faint on the way because you will be coming back with your empty stomach and empty pockets."*

# WORSHIP THROUGH THE STORM

Unperturbed the student went on his way singing and came into the office where he was hoping to get an appointment. On entering the office, still in a joyous mood, he could not help but notice the unhappy countenance of the receptionist seated behind the reception desk. He decided to tell a few jokes to cheer her up, finishing it off with comments on her lovely uniform and beautiful hairstyle. She instantly snapped out of her moodiness and gave the boy the equivalent of £15. It was enough to restock his food supply for a whole month, and still he had some money left over.

This student's story is just another example of what can happen when we choose to worship through the storm. By worshipping God, we are refusing the negative circumstance permission to prevent us from encountering the blessings He has reserved for us.

If we are to encounter the power of worship, we must get rid of the distraction of the present moment. We must make a conscious effort to keep our focus on God and worship Him for Who He is, for His faithfulness to His word and for His love for us. When we do that, our worship sets in motion a display of the splendour of God's Kingdom. It gives us a close-up encounter with His majesty, a revealing of His matchless wisdom, glory, honour, power and authority.

An encounter with the power of worship is exemplified, again, in the life of Stephen in the book of Acts. In the face of bitter opposition, he turned his face towards heaven and worshipped, even thou he was being stoned to death. In so doing, the door of God's presence was flung wide open, and Stephen saw the glory of the Father.

*55 But Stephen, full of the Holy Spirit, looked up to heaven and saw the glory of God, and Jesus standing at the right hand of God. 56 "Look," he said, "I see heaven open and the Son of Man standing at the right hand of God."*

**Acts 7:55-56**

God has not changed; He is the same yesterday today and forever. When we worship, we encounter Him. He opens our eyes to see a new dimension of His glory and to experience His awesomeness.

# Chapter 15

# Responding to the Storm

*Don't be carried away by your circumstances, good or bad;*
*look in front of you and look up.*

When we unexpectedly find ourselves in a storm, it is best not to panic or over-react - as we are naturally predisposed to doing. This is very critical, because when we are in a state of panic, we miss vital clues and critical moments, because our minds have been clouded by fear.

The Bible consistently admonishes us not to give in to fear, mentioning the phrase *"fear not"* 365 times. We are not to entertain fear, but rather to create a room for God's peace by raising an altar of worship. Fear is dangerous; it robs us of the most vital equipment for weathering the storm.

*6 Be anxious for nothing, but in everything by prayer and supplication, with thanksgiving, let your requests be made known to God; 7 and the peace of God, which surpasses all understanding, will guard your hearts and minds through Christ Jesus.*

**Philippians 4:6-7 (NKJV)**

Peace is one of God's ways of equipping us, as believers, to be in the storm but to live outside of it. God's peace allows us to experience His presence in the midst of chaos. His peace keeps

# WORSHIP THROUGH THE STORM

us from being consumed or letting the storm determine our actions. In hindsight, you will realize that fear and ignorance have been the greatest robbers in all of history. Fear renders a person immobile in the face of the storm, whilst the courage of faith empowers one to worship God in spite of the storm. The apostle Paul, in his letter to Timothy, his young apprentice, admonished him, saying:

*⁷ For God has not given us a spirit of fear, but of power and of love and of a sound mind.*

**2 Timothy 1:7 (NKJV)**

It takes a far greater level of faith to worship God through the storm than it takes to pray and fast for Him to cause the storm to cease.

We should not allow fear to drive us into the panic mode of putting our need before God's need. Our need is comfort, but God's need is worship. We should make a deliberate choice to give God what He most desires of us, and then He will take care of every one of our needs. The storm can cloud our minds, making us forget the truth that it is God who made both us and the storm. If only we would keep ourselves in remembrance of this and learn to give Him worship, then we would not need to do any other thing except apply the truths that He has revealed to us.

When we choose to respond to the storm by switching to the worship mode, we become equipped to see various possibilities. We begin to recognise the opportunities for growth and expansion that come with the storm. Thus, we are pre-occupied with what we stand to gain through the storm, not what we might lose. Ironically some people get so fearful of losing what they have that they fail to take the risk to discover who they were uniquely created by God to become.

# Epilogue

*Your faith is only as strong as the test it survives.*

The last four years have been the most challenging in my life, yet, paradoxically, the most rewarding. This is testament to the fact that oftentimes our most valuable treasures are hidden in storms.

During this period, I have been able to do much with very little. Like the prophet Elijah during the time of famine, God has continually supplied my needs. He has sustained my life by the daily provision of a raven-sized meal.

The most exciting part of it is that, not only has He protected my life, He has - most importantly - turned my face towards Him. He has caused my eyes to look upon His face and to discover His purpose for my life. He has set me in the path of the pursuit of divine purpose. This book you are reading is proof of that fact.

Just at the onset of the financial crisis in 2008, I lost my job. This was further complicated by immigration issues. The pain of losing my source of livelihood and the resulting hardship that ensued was excruciating. I was in a storm.

On the other hand, this same storm has served the purpose of helping me to discover life's greatest treasures. I have been able to identify and clarify my purpose for being on earth. The process has helped me to find and develop my unique gifts and talents. Most of all, I have learnt to trust in God. The song

# WORSHIP THROUGH THE STORM

writer Andrae Crouch said it best: *"Through it all, I have learnt to trust in Jesus ... to depend upon His word."*

Through the storm, God has taught me how to divide His Word. I have found treasures hidden in God's Word that would otherwise have remained hidden. God has opened my eyes and got them fixed on Him and not on my skills, abilities or resources. Some of my innate talents and dormant potential have been activated, and are now being put through the process of refinement. I have written several songs, discovered several principles and planned for several years ahead. The storm has served as a catalyst for releasing me into my purpose and passion.

This very moment, as I write, I am praising God for this opportunity to write my first book on a topic based on my primary passion in life: worship. Since my teens, I had been nursing the idea of writing a book based on the interesting story of my Dad's life. I would never have imagined writing a book on worship, using my own personal life experience.

My final word to you is this: *"be encouraged."* Use this stormy period to discover God's heart through worship. Discover His purpose for you and, finally, discovery and develop your inborn gifts and talents. The instant you start pursuing your divine assignment, no matter what type and category of storm it is, God will give you a song. You will literally find a song in your mouth.

Turn your face towards heaven and keep your eyes on Him. Allow worship to flow from your spirit, to your mind and out of your mouth to God. Ask the Holy Spirit to kindle your spirit and teach your heart to worship. Then watch what happens next.

Right in the eye of the storm, where others normally give up or break down, you will see remarkable changes. You will soon start experiencing peace and fulfilment, as you follow the process and continue to worship God. The result of doing this will be increasing levels of peace. This peace will give birth to joy and an unexplainable experience of the Father's love and heart towards you. Unimaginable levels of satisfaction will then envelope your soul, as the door of His presence opens to you. And as you ascend into His presence, you will begin to see and experience new dimensions of His glory.

Practice worshipping through your storm, and you will have discovered the secret door to experiencing peace in the most unusual places in life. When faced with a life-threatening issue, such as a storm, it may seem foolish, in the natural, to choose to worship God rather than putting up a fight through something like warfare prayers. But, so also is every other supernatural wisdom, when seen with earthly eyes. By earthly eyes I mean: your physical eyes.

*14 But the natural man does not receive the things of the Spirit of God, for they are foolishness to him; nor can he know them, because they are spiritually discerned.*

**1 Corinthians 2:14 (NKJV)**

Robe yourself in the garment of worship and get your praise going. Put on your dancing shoes, open your mouth, and sing out loud till the joy of the Lord overflows your heart, and His peace flows like a river from within your soul. And remember: worship is more than words and songs. When you have truly worshipped, you will have truly loved, loving God first and loving your neighbour as yourself, for therein lays your victory. I would like to close by leaving you with these few scriptures to ponder on:

*1 My heat is confident in You o God, no wonder I can sing Your praises with all my heart.*

**Psalm 108:1**

# WORSHIP THROUGH THE STORM

*33 I will sing to the LORD as long as I live;*
*I will sing praise to my God while I have my being.*
*34 May my meditation be sweet to Him;*
*I will be glad in the LORD.*

**Psalm 104:33-34 (NKJV)**


*6 So be truly glad: there is wonderful joy ahead even though you have to endure many trials for a little while. 7 These trials will show that your faith is genuine when your faith remains strong through many trials [storms] it will bring much praise and glory and honour [worship] on the day when Christ is revealed to the world.*

**1 Peter 1:6-7 (NLT)**


*3 Endure suffering [storms] … as a good soldier of Christ Jesus … . 12 If we endure hardship we will also reign with Him.*

**2 Timothy 2:3 and 12 (NLT)**

*25 Look straight ahead and fix your eyes on what lies before you. 26 Mark out a straight path for your feet; stay on the safe path, don't get side-tracked. 27 Turn not to the right hand nor to the left: remove thy foot from evil.*

**Proverbs 4:25-27 (NLT)**

*1 Therefore we also, since we are surrounded by so great a cloud of witnesses, let us lay aside every weight, and the sin which so easily ensnares us, and let us run with endurance the race that is set before us, 2 looking unto Jesus, the author and finisher of our faith, who for the joy that was set before Him endured the cross [storms], despising the shame, and has sat down at the right hand of the throne of God.*

**Hebrews 12:1-2 (NKJV)**

*12 People can never predict when hard times [storms] might come. Like fish in a net or birds in a trap, people are caught by sudden tragedy.*

**Ecclesiastes 9:12 (NLT)**

*10 Don't long for "the good old days." This is not wise. 13 Accept the way God does things … . 14 Enjoy prosperity while you can, but when the hard times [storms] strike, realize that both come from God. Remember that nothing is certain in life.*

**Ecclesiastes 7:10 and 13-14 (NLT)**

*23 But the hour cometh, and now is, when the true worshippers shall* **worship the Father in spirit and in truth:** *for the Father seeketh such to worship him. 24 God is a Spirit: and they that worship him must worship him in spirit and in truth.*

**John 4:23-24 (KJV)**

For Testimonies and Updates Visit:

**www.WorshipThroughTheStorm.com**